Dover Opera Guide and Libretto Series

AÏDA

By

GIUSEPPE VERDI

Translated and Introduced By
ELLEN H. BLEILER

DOVER PUBLICATIONS, INC.
New York

Published in Canada by General Publishing Company, Ltd., 30 Lesmill Road, Don Mills, Toronto, Ontario.
Published in the United Kingdom by Constable and Company, Ltd., 10 Orange Street, London WC 2.

This Dover edition, first published in 1962, contains the following material:
The standard authorized Italian libretto of *Aida*, as originally published by G. Ricordi & Company.
A new English translation of the libretto and supplementary material by Ellen H. Bleiler.

Library of Congress Catalog Card Number: 62-52761

Manufactured in the United States of America
Dover Publications, Inc.
180 Varick Street
New York, N.Y. 10014

CONTENTS

THE COMPOSER

During the early nineteenth century, the Duchy of Parma in northern Italy was one of numerous political prizes claimed and subjugated alternately by the usually embattled French and Austrian Empires. In 1813, the French held the area. Thus it was that the newborn son of one Carlo Verdi, an innkeeper and vendor of groceries and wine in the tiny village of Le Roncole, happened to be registered as Joseph Fortunin François. The baby made his appearance on October 10, 1813. Had he been born one year later (as he, until his middle age, believed to be the case), his birth certificate would have been in German rather than French. For in 1814, Austrian and Russian troops swept over Italy, and, so the story goes, the poor innkeeper's wife and infant son would surely have been at the invaders' mercy but for the young woman's presence of mind; with the baby in her arms, she fled to the village church and hid high in its steeple until the troops left. Signora Luigia Verdi's escape helped shape the course of world music, and a placard on the front of Le Roncole's church commemorates the event. The rescued baby, however, himself never mentioned the episode in later years. As several of his biographers have commented, the story is apocryphal but symbolic: even in infancy, Verdi rose above the feuds and quarrels of lesser men than he.

Little distinguished the early childhood of Giuseppe Verdi from that of any other peasant lad in the area. The parish priest undertook the boy's earliest education; and from a very young age Verdi was enchanted by the tunes of traveling minstrels and players who passed through Le Roncole and sometimes stayed at his father's inn. He begged to be allowed to have music lessons; but delight in songs and melodies are so innate in Italians that probably no one took the little boy's pleas for anything but a passing whim.

When Verdi was six or seven, an incident occurred which made his father reconsider. Giuseppe was serving as an acolyte in the local church, and once, during the performance of his duties, grew so absorbed in the organ music being played that he neglected to hand the priest the holy water. The priest repeated his request for water several times, to no avail. At length the man of God grew impatient with the absent-minded acolyte and tumbled him rather roughly down the church steps. Tearful and bruised, small Verdi returned home; the only statement that could be extracted from him was still another plea to be taught music. And so an ancient, decrepit, and out-of-tune spinet became part of the Verdi household. A neighbor, Stefano Cavaletti, was hired to tune the instrument; Cavaletti, noting the little boy's tremendous pleasure and eagerness in learning to play the old spinet, refused payment for his services. Inside the instrument he left a note stating that young Giuseppe Verdi's interest was adequate reward. The spinet, still containing Cavaletti's words, reposes in a Milan museum.

Le Roncole's organist gave Verdi his first music lessons. In a few years, pupil's skill surpassed master's, and the boy was able to earn a little money by playing the organ at local Masses, weddings, and the like. Carlo Verdi was proud of his son's proficiency, and when the boy was about ten, realized that Giuseppe could be taught little more in Le Roncole; further instruction would have to be sought elsewhere. The elder Verdi discussed this problem with Antonio Barezzi, a well-to-do grocer and business acquaintance who lived in Busseto, a few miles away. Barezzi advised the inn-keeper to enter his son in Busseto's school, and to let the boy continue his music lessons in that town. Probably young Giuseppe had accompanied his father on previous trips to Busseto, and Barezzi had observed the boy's unusual fondness for music. The Busseto merchant must have been both pleased and impressed; for music was, without a doubt, the reigning interest of his own life.

Antonio Barezzi was a remarkable man in any case. Few composers have had Verdi's luck in finding patrons and sponsors whose astuteness, generosity, and unwavering faith enabled their protégés to stick uncompromisingly to their chosen careers, regardless of what misfortunes befell them. Barezzi presided over Busseto's Philharmonic Society, whose rehearsals took place in his home. He himself was an accomplished performer on several instruments and took a lively interest in the musical questions of the day. He kept his eye on the Le Roncole lad, whose talents he soon hoped to use on behalf of the Busseto Philharmonic in a step toward what, Barezzi felt sure, would create considerable local renown.

At first, Verdi lived in the home of a Busseto shoemaker. Rather grudgingly he attended classes at the local high school, where he seems to have done well; in every spare moment, until late at night, he practised on the battered spinet which had accompanied him. His music teacher was Ferdinando Provesi, Busseto's choirmaster and organist as well as a proficient musical theorist. Under Provesi, Verdi progressed so rapidly that quite a spirited competition arose between school teacher and music master as to whose instruction should have precedence over the boy. Verdi presently began to take over some of Provesi's chores. The local population admired the boy's musicianship; even the school teacher agreed that he had talent. At length, Verdi moved into the Barezzi home. He gave piano lessons to Barezzi's daughter Margherita, who was a year or two younger than himself; he learned to play other instruments besides piano, and arranged music for the Philharmonic's concerts. He even found time to compose some pieces, which were praised by Barezzi and other members of the Philharmonic. When he was sixteen, Verdi applied for the post of organist in another town. He was turned down, and stayed in Busseto, continuing to study and practise. But both Barezzi and Provesi realized that once again the boy had mastered all he could be taught locally. In order to continue his musical education, he must seek yet further afield. At the same time, Signora Barezzi began to suspect that the warm friendship between her daughter and Verdi was not entirely the result of their common interest in music. All in all, it might be best if Giuseppe were absent from Busseto for a while. The Milan Conservatory seemed to be the next step; but how on earth could an almost penniless peasant lad ever hope to reach this dazzling Mecca?

At Barezzi's suggestion, Verdi appealed to Busseto's Monte di Pietà for financial aid. The Monte di Pietà was a centuries-old charity, founded to assist the local poor and help their children get otherwise unattainable educations. It must have been difficult for Verdi to make his appeal, no matter how badly he needed the money. He already possessed those personality traits for which he was famous in later years: fanatical honesty and an odd mixture, on the one hand, of painful shyness, and reserve about himself, his background, and his achievements; on the other hand, a quick temper, and an almost fierce stubbornness about his musical integrity and aims. Those who knew Verdi often observed that he retained, throughout his long life, many of both the good and bad traits typical of the peasant stock from which he was descended.

Considerable delay ensued before the Monte di Pietà's directors decided to give Verdi a subsidy. Meanwhile Barezzi had offered to advance twice the amount of the Busseto charity. The high school Latin master armed his erstwhile student with an introduction to a Milanese relation with whom Verdi could live. Permission to travel was obtained, and in the spring of 1832, Giuseppe Verdi, age eighteen, went to Milan to seek admission to the famed Music Conservatory.

There has been a great deal of tumult and shouting about the Conservatory's refusal to admit Verdi. Countless recriminations have been heaped on the heads of the school's faculty; the board of examiners has been charged with everything from merciless snobbery (one of the masters was said to have based his refusal on the fact that he disliked Verdi's looks)* to extraordinary obtuseness (how could any group of music-minded dignitaries fail to recognize that in thirty years this youth would be Italy's foremost operatic composer?). In reality, Verdi was turned down for quite proper reasons: he was eighteen years old, and the Milan Conservatory admitted paying students from the "provinces" over the age of fourteen only in very rare instances—chiefly when the applicant showed really exceptional skill and promise in every part of the examination. Verdi's piano technique was judged faulty—he seems to have overreached himself in the choice of

---

* The passport with which Verdi traveled from Busseto to Milan described him as tall, thin-faced and pock-marked, with chestnut-colored hair, gray eyes, an aquiline nose, and a small beard.

View of Le Roncole. The house at the extreme left is the one in which Verdi was born in 1813. Also shown is the church in which Luigia Verdi is said to have taken refuge with her child when Austrian and Russian troops overran the town.

(Gatti, Carlo: *Verdi nelle Immagini.* Published by Garzanti, Milan, 1941)

(Verdi nelle Immagini)

Ferdinando Provesi, Verdi's first music teacher.

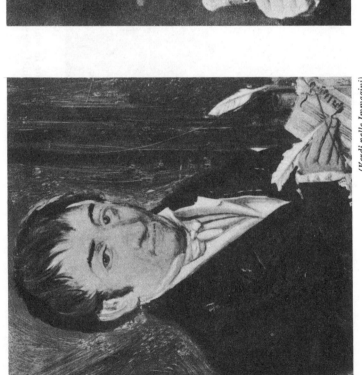

(Verdi nelle Immagini)

Antonio Barezzi, Verdi's patron at Busseto, later his father-in-law.

(Verdi nelle Immagini)

Giovanni Ricordi, later the world's greatest music publisher. His foresight and interest aided the young Verdi.

(Verdi nelle Immagini)

Bartolomeo Merelli, impresario at La Scala. He produced *Un Giorno di Regno, Nabucco,* and *I Lombardi.*

Margherita Barezzi, Verdi's first wife.

selections he played for the examiners; he had applied for admission as a student of composition, but he himself, many years later, confessed that the musical samples he submitted to the judges were less than good. Whatever the reasons, the Conservatory's refusal to admit Verdi seemed irrevocable, and the young man was advised to further his career via private instruction. Depressed, but with no thought of abandoning his ambition, Verdi became a pupil of Vincenzo Lavigna, a Conservatory teacher and minor official* at the opera, who also gave private lessons. For Verdi, Lavigna's instruction was the final step in his student career.

The choice of Lavigna was fortunate. This man greatly admired seventeenth- and eighteenth-century music. Though primarily an opera composer himself, he gave his pupil a thorough knowledge of the classic harmony and counterpoint in the works of early masters like Palestrina. Verdi never forgot these lessons. Many years later, on one of the few occasions when he advised fledgling musicians, he urged them to follow a similar course of study. Throughout his entire career, Verdi referred to and used the basic musical techniques Lavigna taught him.

Aware of his indebtedness to Antonio Barezzi, and determined to repay his benefactor as soon as possible, Verdi drove himself mercilessly for the next two years. Occasionally he managed to attend an opera at La Scala. In his quiet persistent way, he must have mused about these performances and absorbed ideas from them. But it was a lucky coincidence which first turned him to the actual composing of an opera.

Pleased at his pupil's progress, Lavigna introduced him to a number of prominent impresarios and musicians. Among these men was Pietro Massini, who, in about April 1834, was overseeing a performance of Haydn's "Creation" at Milan's Philodramatic Theater. Verdi was urged to attend a rehearsal. On the evening that he went, none of the conductors hired to lead the work appeared. Massini doubted his own musical abilities, and seeing his friend Lavigna's timid student, asked him if he could just accompany a little at the piano and wave his hands at the chorus, so that the rehearsal might get under way. Verdi obliged; the

* Known at La Scala as *maestro al cembalo* whose duties are considerably more varied than that of the American prompter.

rehearsal was so successful and won such praise from the performers that Verdi was asked to conduct the actual performance. This too was a triumph; Milan's Austrian commandant and local nobility even ordered it repeated. Because of this success Verdi received a commission to compose a cantata for a Milan aristocrat and was subsequently asked by Massini not only to conduct other works at the Philodramatic Theater, but to write an opera for production on its stage. For the latter purpose, Verdi was even provided with a libretto.

Just when everything seemed to be going well in Milan, Verdi learned to his sorrow that his former teacher, Provesi of Busseto, had died. The posts of organist and choirmaster in Busseto were now officially vacant, and Verdi was urged to return promptly and apply for them. Pleased by the prospect of seeing Margherita Barezzi and her father again, Verdi went back to Busseto, taking his opera libretto with him. On the day he returned, Busseto's ecclesiastical party, never very enthusiastic toward Verdi, arbitrarily and without examination appointed someone else to fill the jobs which Verdi wanted.

A noisy, prolonged, and bitter brawl now broke out between Busseto's citizens and the clergy. The pro-Verdi citizenry felt its candidate for the organist-choirmaster post was by far the most suitable and best-trained, and had been dealt with in grossly unfair manner. The clerical party just as heatedly insisted on retaining the man already appointed, whose initial recommendation had come from the Bishop himself. The citizens boycotted the Cathedral and played Verdi's music in the town square; the clergy tried to outlaw the Philharmonic Society. Tempers flared to such an extent that the government had to step in. It was presently announced that a fair and open competition for the position of Music Master of Busseto would be held—but no date was set. Verdi, discouraged and in financial straits, asked Lavigna to help him find a position elsewhere, which Lavigna did. Busetto's pro-Verdi faction, hearing of their candidate's impending departure, accused him of desertion and ingratitude (after all, they had helped pay for his musical education). Verdi was in a quandary; if he waited much longer, both his job prospects might vanish. Finally, however, the long awaited Busseto competition did take place. Verdi won easily. (His opponents' candidate never showed up and was replaced by a last-minute substitute.) Verdi was now officially Master of Music to the Commune of Busseto. The whole bothersome affair had three major effects upon his career: first, he was able to marry Margherita Barezzi in 1836 with Antonio's blessings and pecuniary aid; second, impetus was given to his life-long dislike of the clergy; and third, he finally managed to get to work on his opera, *Oberto, Conte di San Bonifacio*. This is the earliest of Verdi's operas for which the score still exists. The composer's letters from this period speak of another work, *Rocester*, but this may have been merely an early draft of *Oberto*.

Verdi worked on *Oberto* for two or three years—a long time for the man who later composed his best-known works within three or four months. In 1837, a daughter was born to the young couple; fifteen months later, a son. Meanwhile, Verdi corres-ponded with Massini in Milan; the latter promised to see what he could do about getting *Oberto* produced. This project presented some difficulties, for Massini was no longer director of the Philo-dramatic Theater. Massini, however, both as a tribute to the memory of the recently deceased Lavigna, and because he was genuinely impressed by Verdi's talents, reached Signor Barto-lomeo Merelli, who had recently become impresario at La Scala. Complex negotiations ensued; Verdi plodded back and forth be-tween Busseto and Milan. Finally, rehearsals of *Oberto* began—only to halt when a leading member of the cast fell ill. Verdi's troubles were not only professional: soon after the birth of the second child, his little girl died; and only a year or so later, his son died too.*

Deeply saddened, the Verdis had moved to Milan after the first death. For a large part of their livelihood, they were still dependent upon the kindness and generosity of the good Antonio Barezzi.

---

* For a long time, it was thought that all three deaths—Verdi's daughter, son, and wife—occurred within three months, while the composer worked on *Un Giorno di Regno*. This belief was apparently founded on a statement by Verdi himself, but his recollection of dates—even vital ones in his own life—was none too accurate. Verdi not infrequently mentioned an event as having happened at one time, when careful documented evidence shows it un-doubtedly must have taken place at another. Verdi's little girl died in 1838, while the family was still in Busseto; the little boy, just before the Milan pro-duction of *Oberto*, in 1839; and his wife, Margherita, died in June of the following year.

Personal tragedy and professional trials did not diminish Verdi's
stubborn pride and financial honor. He never regarded Barezzi's
assistance either as his just due, or as outright gifts. Dutifully and
promptly, he wrote promissory notes for each loan and, he was
finally able to repay both his father-in-law and the community of
Busseto for their aid.

The production of *Oberto* might well have been dropped entirely
if some of La Scala's top singers had not praised the music to
Impresario Merelli after a rehearsal. (One of these singers was
Giuseppina Strepponi, a leading soprano of the day, who would
eventually become Verdi's almost perfect second wife.) Merelli
listened to his singers, and rehearsals for *Oberto* began afresh.
Finally, in 1839, the opera was produced at La Scala, where it was
successful enough to be repeated thirteen times that season—and
where it was heard by a shrewd gentleman named Ricordi, who
had already begun his own meteoric career as a music publisher, and
who added *Oberto* to a list of works for which he had bought rights.

Giovanni Ricordi was known as a man of unusually keen
artistic insight and an uncanny ability to foresee success or failure,
commercial and artistic, for a musical work. For some years he
was an important figure in the world of Italian opera. In a few
decades, Ricordi was to become the world's most important music
publisher. Ricordi's interest in Verdi, plus the latter's fair triumph
with his first opera, convinced Merelli to give Verdi a contract to
compose several more operas for La Scala.

A comic libretto, *Un Giorno di Regno* ("A Day's Reign"), was
selected. Verdi was not entirely happy with the choice—violent
action and melodrama, with one exception, would always be more
to his taste—but he began to compose anyway. Little money was
left from the sale of *Oberto*; the rent was due; there was no time to
get another loan from Busseto; and Verdi was loath to ask Merelli
for an advance. Precious time was lost when Verdi became too
sick to compose. Margherita sold a few trinkets she still owned to
pay the rent, over which Verdi had worried and fretted. At last,
when he was able to resume work, Margherita had an attack of
encephalitis and died within a few days. And Giuseppe Verdi,
twenty-six years old, nearly penniless, deprived of his family, one
after the other in rapid and tragic succession, had about eight
weeks in which to complete a comic opera.

Interior and exterior views of La Scala Opera House, Milan, circa 1845.

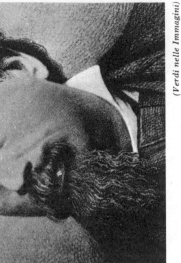

Amilcare Ponchielli

Arrigo Boito

Composers contemporary with Verdi. Boito, composer of *Mefistofele*, supplied the superb librettos for Verdi's *Otello* and *Falstaff*. Ponchielli wrote the famous *La Gioconda*.

Francesco Maria Piave, Verdi's librettist for *Ernani*, *Rigoletto*, and *Un Ballo in Maschera*.

Jenny Lind, world-famous soprano who sang the lead in the première of Verdi's *I Masnadieri* in London in 1847.

Verdi and Giuseppina Strepponi, circa 1848.

Un Giorno di Regno was performed in September 1840. It was a complete failure. The event left an indelible mark on Verdi—he never forgot it. Proud and independent, he was pleased throughout the rest of his career to accept public approval or condemnation stoically and uncomplainingly. He offered his works for judgment solely on artistic merit, and he could accept praise or ridicule with equal dignity. But the audience's reaction to *Un Giorno di Regno* hurt and embittered him. A nineteenth-century Milan opera enthusiast fed on gossip about artists and musicians in much the same way as a twentieth-century movie-goer depends upon Hollywood fan magazines. Verdi's misfortunes were common knowledge. Perhaps it was the only time in his life that he felt his personal circumstances should have influenced the critics' harsh consensus and at least, he later wrote, the audience could have paid him the courtesy of quiet attention. Instead, it actually hissed and made jokes about the opera. As a result of the whole affair, Verdi resolved to withdraw from his contract with Merelli. With stubborn finality, he made up his mind never to compose again.

Operas were common and much-demanded entertainment in nineteenth-century Italy. Hundreds of them were written. Every major Italian city and town had its own opera house and orchestra; strolling troupes of singers and actors brought new works to the outlying villages. If an audience disliked a particular opera, small matter; it would approve the next one. Impresario Merelli knew this; he tried hard to convince Verdi of it, urging him not to be discouraged by one failure—ample future successes would surely atone for it. Verdi was adamant, he was through with opera. His musical endeavours, henceforth, would be confined to teaching. Merelli was an unusual man in a profession that is not generally associated with the virtue of exemplary patience. He did not lose his temper at Verdi; he did not upbraid him for breach of contract. But a few months later, he requested Verdi to read and comment on a new libretto about the Biblical King Nebuchadnezzar. Many years later Verdi recalled how that evening he had grudgingly taken the libretto home with him and tossed it angrily on the table. Inadvertently, his eyes rested upon the words, "*Va pensiero, sull'ali dorate*" ("Go, thought on golden wings.") Fascinated by these lines, Verdi read the libretto many times in succession until he virtually knew it by heart. The next day he returned it to Merelli, mentioning that he thought it was excellent. Merelli urged him to set it to music; Verdi refused. Merelli thrust the libretto at him, pushed him out of the room, and locked the door. Verdi went home and began to compose.

The work progressed so fast that Merelli agreed to put it on at La Scala the coming Carnival Season. But when the prospectus of Scala productions was issued, *Nabucco** was not mentioned. Verdi penned a furious note to Merelli—and instead of tearing it up, as he later ruefully admitted he should have—sent it to the impresario. The next morning, Merelli summoned Verdi. Trembling, the young composer arrived, afraid his hot temper and rash words had permanently blighted his career. Patiently and reasonably, Merelli explained the reason for *Nabucco's* omission from the Scala prospectus: three other new operas had previously been promised for the Carnival Season, and a fourth new production would simply be too expensive. However, if Verdi were willing to have *Nabucco* presented with available old props and costumes, Merelli would produce it. Relieved and grateful, Verdi agreed. A new Scala prospectus was issued, including *Nabucco*. Singers were chosen. (For the second time, Giuseppina Strepponi's name appears in connection with Verdi's work). *Nabucco* received its première, after less than two weeks of rehearsals, on March 9, 1842. It was an instantaneous success. Within a few days, Verdi's name became a byword all over Italy.

The next opera, *I Lombardi alla prima crociata* ("The Lombards at the First Crusade"), appeared less than a year later. Its production marked the first of Verdi's conflicts with censorship—conflicts which arose regularly in following years. In the case of *I Lombardi*, the librettist was suspected of basing his text on a book which was banned because it expressed nationalist sentiments. Composer, librettist, and La Scala Impresario Merelli were summoned by the chief of police. Verdi coolly ignored the summons—the authorities could either accept the opera as he had written it or not at all. Merelli urgently pleaded that stage, scenery, and singers were completely set for the opera. The police chief wavered and backed down; he dictated one change so minor that even Verdi

---

* The opera is actually named *Nabucodonosor*, but Verdi himself nicknamed it *Nabucco*, and the latter title is by far the better known.

could not object to it, and the opera was performed. It mattered little whether this particular charge was true or not; a restless public, sick of foreign domination and longing for an Italy united under one ruler, had already identified its sentiments with those of the Jewish captives in *Nabucco*; the same public was equally keen to see in a story of medieval Lombardy's military prowess an expression of current patriotism. Despite police surveillance at the première, *I Lombardi* was a roaring success. Verdi's name began to have a dual significance throughout Italy. Whenever one of his operatic characters proclaimed against tyranny and oppression— whether or not their source in the opera was political—it was regarded as a veiled declaration of Italian patriotism. Verdi (whose personal sympathies were frankly for Italian independence and unity) became a symbol. Some years later, up and down the peninsula, the words "*Viva Verdi*" would be scrawled again and again on walls and streets by a resourceful populace. How could officialdom protest a music loving nation's praise for its current celebrity? It was only sheer coincidence that the letters V-E-R-D-I also stood for "*Vittorio Emmanuele, Re d'Italia*" ("Victor Emmanuel, King of Italy"), a nationalist slogan.

Verdi's work is generally divided into three periods. The operas of the first period (1839–1849) are the most numerous—fifteen.* Those of the second period (1850–1867) are the most often performed—including such favorites as *Rigoletto* and *Il Trovatore*. And those of the final period—*Otello* (1887) and *Falstaff* (1893)—are the most highly regarded by critics. *Aida* (1871) is usually considered as the bridge between the middle and final periods. In the eleven years following *Oberto*, Verdi created sixteen operas. The earliest of these already displayed the tuneful vigor, sometimes to the point of crudeness, that marked his style. During this period he was less concerned with showing subtle character delineations than with musical expression of violent and melodramatic action on the stage. Verdi wrote music to be sung. He composed with a particular voice and range in mind. His arias and choruses are striking in their musical forthrightness and directness. Verdi himself insisted on accurate interpretation of both words and music by the singers whom he rehearsed. He was a stern and merciless coach, demanding the utmost of every artist who performed his

* Sixteen, if *Jérusalem*, French version of *I Lombardi*, is counted.

works. Rehearsals under Verdi's supervision were practically guaranteed to separate the men from the boys. Mediocre singers feared and hated his acid criticism and his relentless drive toward perfection; first-rate singers perspired, complained, repeated the music until they were ready to fling their scores in the composer's face, finally admitting that they had never sounded better and had been unaware of their own potentialities.

In 1844, with the opera *Ernani* (regarded unkindly by Victor Hugo, on whose play the work was based), Verdi began his long collaboration with the librettist Francesco Piave. This gentle, affable versifier was a Venetian, the resident poet of his native city's Fenice theater. First destined for the law, he had found theatrical life more to his taste and ended his career as the author of about sixty opera libretti. Piave is generally ridiculed as a poetaster and writer of doggerel. Weaknesses in the operas on which he collaborated are often attributed to his silly libretti. But this is less Piave's fault than many critics claim. Verdi chose his own plots, with a decided bias for such extreme violence and melodramatic complexities that they often border on the ludicrous. Piave cheerfully acknowledged the superiority of the composer's work to his own. Verdi knew precisely what he wanted from his mild-mannered librettist and told him so in no uncertain terms— sometimes down to the last strophe and syllable. Piave unquestioningly complied, without worrying about the possible misuse of his own literary art. The association lasted for twenty years and included the most famous middle-period operas. The pair formed an interesting contrast to composers like Puccini, whose merciless bullying frequently drove his librettists to utter fury and despair; or to Richard Wagner, who found *all* librettists so monstrously unsatisfactory that he ended up writing his own texts.

Verdi grew very fond of Piave, never criticizing or ridiculing him for work which had provoked adverse comment about an opera. In 1867, Piave had a stroke which left him totally unable to move for eight years before his death. Verdi paid a large part of the medical expenses; and he not only aided directly in the support of the librettist's family but also spent much time and effort in persuading five other composers to collaborate with him on a song book whose royalties were to go to Piave's young daughter.

On the whole, the years following *Ernani* were busy and satisfying ones for Verdi. His fame spread; London and Paris began to know his work. Between 1844 and 1851 he managed to compose thirteen more operas, and also traveled up and down Italy helping to stage his works in the many theaters which clamored for them. In 1847 *Macbeth*, generally acclaimed by Verdi and his critics as his best early work, was produced in Florence. Verdi admired Shakespeare above all other dramatists; for some time, he considered *King Lear* as the subject of an opera, and made a prose outline for a libretto. (*Hamlet* and *The Tempest* were two other plays whose operatic possibilities interested him.)

Macbeth was a work especially dear to Verdi. For this reason he dedicated it to Antonio Barezzi, who, as proud as ever of his protégé, made a special trip to Florence to see the opera. The work was something of a novelty for its day: a baritone, not a tenor, sang the lead; the plot contained no love story; and the opera's main characters were also its villains. Almost twenty years later, Verdi still cared enough for *Macbeth* to revise it thoroughly and painstakingly for the Paris Opéra. In late February of 1847, Verdi arrived in Florence to direct rehearsals. Partly because of his affection for the work, and perhaps because he was still recovering from a bad bout of the stomach trouble he periodically suffered, Verdi drove the cast with even more than his customary relentless discipline. When a singer complained that he had already done one hundred and fifty practice runs of a particular piece, he was coolly informed by the composer that if such were the case he would kindly do the hundred and fifty-first. *Macbeth* had a fine public reception. The Florentine audience gleefully seized on Macduff's exhortation to his Scottish comrades-in-arms as still another patriotic battle-cry. Some time later in Venice, at another performance of *Macbeth*, the police had to be called in to quell the ensuing riot—not an uncommon event after a Verdi opera.

Shortly after *Macbeth's* première, Verdi accepted an invitation to London. Even before composing *Macbeth*, he had begun to work on *I Masnadieri* ("The Robbers"),* a new opera which was to have its first performance in that city. He described his trip to London as decidedly uncomfortable, if quite diverting. The city

* Based on *Die Räuber*, a play by Schiller.

itself intrigued him, although he was surprised that the British climate did not permanently impair his health. The première of *I Masnadieri* was attended by all sorts of royalty. Jenny Lind, the current public idol, sang the lead. The performance was quite successful, despite some ill-concealed titters occasioned by a portly member of the cast whose part, unfortunately, called for him to portray a prisoner on the verge of starving to death.

After London, Verdi went to Paris to arrange for translations and performances of his works at the Opéra. Paris, for the moment, offered certain attractions. Verdi, as a personality, was not yet sufficiently well known to suffer the intrusions of his privacy and the glare of publicity that incessantly confronted him at home; but even more interesting to the composer, Giuseppina Strepponi had retired from an active career on stage to teach singing in Paris. The first attraction was soon canceled by the success at the Paris Opéra of *I Lombardi*, or rather, a French revision of that work entitled *Jérusalem*; but the second proved strong enough to keep Verdi in Paris for most of the next year.

Distance did not lessen the composer's interest in Italian politics. Europe seethed in 1848; that February marked the overthrow of the French throne. Verdi, still in Paris, observed the event with detached irony. The next month, however, Milan rose against the Austrians, and after a violent, bloody battle even managed to declare its independence before the Austrians brutally reasserted their power. Verdi hastened to Milan and had to flee from the city when Austrian reprisals began. More and more frequently, the uprisings all over Italy appeared doomed to failure; worse yet, their leaders were in disagreement and squabbled bitterly among themselves. Disgusted both with the situation in Italy and the failure of the French to intervene on behalf of the Italians, Verdi returned to Paris. He had previously agreed to compose an opera for Rome; now it was almost inevitable that the opera should have a patriotic theme. *La Battaglia di Legnano* ("The Battle of Legnano"), a story of the Lombard League's fight against Frederick Barbarossa, resulted. One of the most notable things about the première of this work seems to have been that it inspired a soldier in the audience to such fervor that he hurled objects down upon the stage from the fourth tier of boxes where he was seated; his missiles included chairs as well as his coat and his sword. In 1959, one hundred and ten years after this first performance, *La Battaglia di Legnano* was revived at the Spoleto Festival.

Perhaps the most important thing Verdi did in 1848 was to purchase the Villa Sant'Agata and its adjoining farm land near Busseto. For more than fifty years, Sant'Agata was to give Verdi the seclusion he desired and the opportunity to manage a thriving and profitable farm as a side occupation. Sant'Agata remains today, much as it was when Verdi lived in it, a national shrine to a famous citizen. While repairs and alterations were in progress at Sant'Agata, Verdi returned to Paris, where he spent almost another full year. In about 1849 he and Madame Strepponi finally began living together openly (they were married in 1859); they remained together for forty-seven years—an ideal relationship.

Giuseppina Strepponi, two years younger than Verdi, was the daughter of a musician. At nineteen she made her singing début and for years was a widely applauded soprano. When her voice began to fail, she became a successful singing teacher in Paris, where she was welcomed enthusiastically by the elite intelligentsia. No intellectual herself, Madame Strepponi possessed a lively intelligence, remarkable insight, sensitivity and tact, a quick ironic wit, great charm, and sufficient musical knowledge to share the interests of Verdi's profession fully. She understood Verdi thoroughly; Madame Strepponi's humor, patience, and tact usually succeeded where the exhortations of theater directors, impresarios, and music publishers failed. She was greatly loved, admired and respected by all Verdi's friends; but perhaps it was inevitable that when she moved into Sant'Agata with him, Busseto eyebrows were raised, and tongues wagged furiously. The town's citizens felt that they had given Verdi his education and his first chance to become famous; now he repaid them not only by behaving in a most unconventional fashion, but also by refusing to offer the slightest explanation or apology for such behavior. Even Antonio Barezzi joined to some extent in this criticism. Verdi was furious. He had long since repaid his financial debt to Busseto; he had fulfilled his moral obligation by bringing to the town the nation's esteem and gratitude. But above all, the composer bitterly resented the interference into his private affairs. He neither pried into nor judged other personal lives; how dare they do so to his? Presently, the storm subsided. Giuseppina Strepponi's endearing qualities won the affection of Busseto. She and Barezzi soon became fast friends.

After 1851, Verdi composed mostly masterpieces. The first of these was commissioned by Venice's Fenice theater. Verdi considered several possible sources for the work and finally chose the least probable one: a Victor Hugo play, *Le Roi s'amuse*, which had been banned from the Paris stage because of its scandalously indecent subject. The story fascinated him, and he was especially intrigued by the dramatic possibilities of its physically and emotionally twisted leading character. From somewhere both Verdi and Piave, who wrote the libretto, received assurances that they would not be hindered by censorship, and their work progressed rapidly. Once Verdi had crystallized his ideas, the actual composition took him forty days. The opera, with the name *La Maledizione* ("The Curse"), which struck certain factions as highly blasphemous, was near completion when the censor stepped in and demanded to see the score. A few days later Verdi and Piave were told that their obscene and revolting work could not possibly be performed. Patiently, Piave toned down the libretto and recast the profligate French king as an obscure prince. Verdi objected to these changes and positively refused to allow any others. The whole point of the opera, he felt, would be lost if the story were watered down. A complete deadlock resulted; finally, one of the censor's men suggested a satisfactory compromise: the story could stand more or less unaltered, but the action must be relocated and the characters renamed. François, the King of France, became a Duke of Mantua; Blanche, his hunchbacked jester's daughter, became Gilda; Triboulet, the jester himself, was rechristened Rigoletto, and the whole work was named for him. That a censor, fearful of the effect such a true story of royal decadence might have on the restless public, could insist on these changes is at least understandable; but the final squabble over *Rigoletto* arose over an absurdly trivial detail. The authorities objected strenuously to the sack in which the dying Gilda is handed to her father. Verdi insisted the sack must stay, arguing that in such matters of theatrical effectiveness he and not the censor must be the judge. At length, another compromise was achieved: the sack could stay, but the lecherous Duke was deprived of the ultimate token of his wretchedness, namely the key to Gilda's room.

In March 1851 *Rigoletto* was performed in Venice. It was so successful that even Verdi, normally the most cautious and reserved of men in judging his own work, realized he had created something which would assure his immortality. Perhaps he had sensed this in advance. There is the widely known story of how Verdi swore the tenor and cast to absolute secrecy about one of the numbers in his forthcoming work, so that there was no possibility of the particular aria's leaking into public ears before the performance. Verdi was right; the day after the première, this aria was ground out by most of Venice's organ grinders, and the rest of Italy speedily picked up the melody. It has since become one of the three or four best-known of all tenor arias, a tune familiar even to those who would never venture inside an opera house. It is "*La donna è mobile*" ("Woman is fickle").

The final tribute to *Rigoletto's* greatness came in rather backhanded fashion from Victor Hugo himself. That venerable, if sometimes stuffy, author bitterly resented Verdi's success with what had once been his own failure. He waged a court battle to prohibit its Paris performance. Hugo lost; after a while, even he changed his mind and became a staunch *Rigoletto* enthusiast.

Verdi spent much of the rest of 1851 in Busseto, continuing to renovate and improve his house and grounds. About this time there was also some correspondence with his publisher Ricordi concerning a decrease in the composer's royalties. Musical pirates had become such a problem that Ricordi found it an expensive matter to prevent wholesale stealing of his property. Verdi agreed to the royalty decreases with some jokes at Ricordi's expense about rich publishers and poor composers. An astute, thrifty businessman, Verdi maintained a keen and active interest in the financial aspects of his work—he enjoyed earning money, but considered any sort of haggling beneath his dignity.

A Spanish play, *El Trovador*, had interested the composer for some time, and he next turned his attention to an operatic version of this. The play itself was a frightful hodgepodge of improbability and wild derring-do, but, as in the case of *Rigoletto*, one character attracted Verdi enough to outweigh the drama's weaknesses. In *El Trovador—Il Trovatore* ("The Troubador"), as it became in Italian—this was the old Gypsy woman, Azucena. Verdi's sympathy for Azucena and her feelings toward her "son" may have been heightened by the death of his mother, which occurred about this time. *Il Trovatore's* libretto was by Salvatore Cammarano, who died unexpectedly before his work was fully completed. Verdi paid Cammarano's widow the full price for the libretto (it was then the custom for a composer to buy his own libretti), and, generous as always, gave her an extra sum besides. *Il Trovatore* enjoyed a successful première in Rome in 1853; so much so that within two years almost every country in Europe, from England to Russia, was performing it. The consensus seemed to be that Verdi's music was good enough to outweigh the deficiencies of plot and libretto.

The next opera was scheduled for Venice's Fenice theater. Verdi, sometime before, had taken a strong dislike to La Scala's management and policies, and much to the dismay of his Milanese publisher, refused to compose for this theater. During a brief trip to Paris, Verdi had seen the younger Dumas's play *La Dame aux Camélias*. He set the work to music, at the same time as *Il Trovatore*, retitling it *La Traviata* ("The Strayed Woman"). Its first performance was in March 1853, only two months after that of *Il Trovatore*. Piave had written an unusually good libretto for it; the work was full of irresistible melodies; the plot quite different from the usual murky Verdian violence. Nevertheless *La Traviata* was the biggest fiasco produced in Venice for years. Its failure on the second night was even worse than on the first.

Many reasons have been offered to explain this debacle. The plot dealt with contemporary morals which may have made the audience slightly uncomfortable. The staging was bad; sophisticated Venetians snickered at what seemed to them a ludicrous attempt at a sumptuous ball. The male singers lost their voices completely, either just before the performance or during it. And the evening's greatest mirth was provoked by the strapping, rosy soprano who was supposed to be dying of consumption right in front of the audience's eyes.

Verdi accepted the debacle calmly. He acknowledged the failure frankly and did not try to pin blame for it on any particular factor. To interested friends he wrote that only time would tell whether the failure had been the fault of his music, the singers, or the production. *La Traviata* was revived a year later; it was an overwhelming success, and, of course, since then has been indispensable to every opera company's repertory. Even today, the

men with work. *Simon Boccanegra*, which he composed during this period, was a comparative failure. (It has never become truly popular, despite an almost complete revision done in 1881.) Verdi, although he felt his music for the work was good, again had no quarrel with the public's judgment. The opinion of music critics mattered little to him. Once, before the première of one of his operas, an enterprising journalist submitted to him two versions of the same review—one favorable, the other not. A small consideration, the journalist hinted, would assure publication of the good review. Verdi shrugged. "Print whatever you like," he said. "It's all the same to me."

All this time, the censors had been active in altering productions of previous Verdi operas, which were being performed throughout Italy. Verdi growled and made furious protests about his works being chopped and butchered to a point where any kind of artistic unity was lost. But the next head-on clash with censorship did not take place until 1858. It was the most violent clash to date, and was caused by a French play, *Gustavus III*, which Verdi was turning into the opera that was to become *Un Ballo in Maschera* ("A Masked Ball"). *Gustavus III* concerns the assassination of a Swedish king, a subject about which the authorities were hypersensitive due to a recent attempt on the life of Napoleon III of France. The censor's men tried to rewrite Piave's entire libretto. Verdi refused to allow their changes. The people of Naples, where the opera was to be performed, were so aroused by the conflict that riots occurred over the question. More than ever, Verdi became a symbol for Italian nationalism and unity. The matter was finally settled when Verdi allowed the opera's action to be transferred to Puritan Boston (about as inappropriate a choice for *Un Ballo's* goings-on as could possibly have been made). Finally, in February 1859, the opera was successfully and triumphantly staged at Rome. With *Un Ballo in Maschera*, Verdi reached a higher level of artistic accomplishment. The work is usually considered a step above its predecessors—its musical construction and its characterization are the culmination of Verdi's powers to that date, and an indication of the shape his future efforts would take.

In April 1859, Count Cavour's efforts to foment war between Austria and England finally met with success. (Cavour expressed

work conveys emotional impact. To a contemporary a
seeing its own standards of morality enacted before it, the
must have been much greater. One of Verdi's biographei
tions a French lady who attended every single Paris perfoi
of *La Traviata* and found herself so deeply moved at each pe
ance that she could never stay to the end of any one.

Verdi spent the next months of 1853 in further work c
projected *King Lear*. In October, however, he went to Paris f
première of his next work. Verdi was not overly fond of
Paris or the French; the Paris Opéra struck him as something
glorified factory—as it had affected Donizetti and Rossini,
last major Italians who composed for it. But Paris still retaine
status as the center of world culture. Verdi, like his famed
decessors, well knew the value of Parisian acclaim for his car
Thus, in October 1853, Verdi worked hard at the Paris Opéra
assure the success of *I Vespri Siciliani* ("The Sicilian Vespers").
number of factors seemed to be against him; one was that t
French emerged as the work's villains, massacred by the hero
Italian underdogs; another was that just as rehearsals were read
to begin, the leading soprano, a Mademoiselle Cruvelli, vanishe
into thin air, and all efforts to locate her failed. Verdi fretted im
patiently; the whole continent discussed the mystery. Verdi was
about to abandon the whole Parisian project when Cruvelli returned just as suddenly as she had disappeared, blithely explaining
that the person who was supposed to present her excuses to the
Opéra must have forgotten to do so. The reason for her absence,
it seems, was a pressing need for a sort of pre-wedding trip with
the gentleman she later married. All ended well, chiefly because
Cruvelli's first operatic role after her return was a part that called
for her initial appearance on stage to be greeted by the request
that she reveal the outcome of her recent adventurous trip. The
delighted audience roared; Cruvelli was forgiven; rehearsals of
I Vespri Siciliani began; and when presented a few months later,
the opera was a success.

Between 1854 and 1857, besides a few side trips to Paris, Verdi
was usually busy at Sant'Agata, where he had developed a real
passion for farming. He oversaw the harvest and the raising of
livestock; when an economic depression engulfed the surrounding
area, Verdi increased his own operations in order to provide more

his pleasure at the news by bursting into an aria from *Il Trovatore*.) Verdi, still rankling from the storm raised by *Un Ballo in Maschera*, turned his attention almost wholly from music to politics. He raised money to help Italian war victims. When the Austrians were defeated, Verdi was one of those elected to inform Victor Emmanuel that the Duchy of Parma would join the rest of the country in accepting him as its king. The composer did this readily enough. Though basically a republican, Verdi found the realization of a united Italy more important to him than his personal desires. At this time, Verdi finally made the personal acquaintance of Cavour, and the two men regarded one another with mutual esteem until Cavour's death in 1861.

Besides his political activities (which included the devious purchase of hard-to-get guns for the Busseto area, which for some time feared the Austrians' return), Verdi managed to spend most of 1859 and 1860 in happy isolation at Sant'Agata, overseeing farming activities. 1860 marked Garibaldi's famous march, as well as the first convocation of a United Italian Parliament. Cavour persuaded Verdi to sit in the Parliament as Deputy from Busseto— a post Verdi did not greatly relish and hoped to relinquish at the earliest opportunity. (He finally did in 1865.)

The next year (1861), Verdi returned to composing. He had been asked for an opera by the Imperial Theater of St. Petersburg, Russia, and this commission presently resulted in *La Forza del Destino* ("The Force of Destiny"). Toward the end of the year, the Verdis made the long trip to Russia to supervise the production; but at the last moment the leading soprano inopportunely fell ill, and Verdi persuaded the management of the Imperial Theater to postpone the work until next season.

From Russia, the Verdis went to London, where an International Exhibition was in progress. The composer had let himself be persuaded to write the "Hymn of Nations" for this Exhibition, as the representative sample of Italian music.

Verdi detested this sort of task—frequently rejecting requests for dedicatory or commemorative music. This time, however, he complied because Italy's other foremost composer, Rossini, had declared himself too old and feeble for the task. The "Hymn of Nations" was hardly a major effort on Verdi's part, though it was well enough received. The words had been written by a very young, very hot-headed Italian poet, Arrigo Boito. It was Boito's first association with Verdi and the beginning of a long, often stormy relationship, that was to culminate in the almost perfect blend of words and music in Verdi's last two operas *Otello* and *Falstaff*.

During early fall of 1862, the peripatetic Verdi returned to Russia, where *La Forza del Destino* was finally performed. The work was fairly successful, although its excessively gloomy and complicated plot seems to have surprised even the Russians, who should have been accustomed to the somber mood.

For the next few years, Verdi was not of the most cheerful disposition. Never particularly gay, except on rare occasions among intimate friends, the Maestro now settled into a long stretch of pessimism. Several factors contributed to this. The political chores, to which he was giving much of his time, did not really stimulate him greatly. He was depressed by what he felt to be a conspicuous lowering of standards in Italy's opera houses—with his own works suffering, as a result. And for all his customary indifference to such matters, he was upset by a rising school of musical criticism which loudly praised the works and theories of Richard Wagner, while belittling Italian opera as it had developed in the nineteenth century. To Verdi, the new critics' opinions were an attack not only on himself, but also on the predecessors whom he still greatly admired, and to whose music he owed so much: Bellini, Donizetti, Rossini.

In 1865, Verdi rather grudgingly agreed to write another opera for Paris. This was *Don Carlos*,* again based on a play by Schiller. The French libretto was written by two young men (Verdi once complained that everybody concerned with the Paris Opéra came in pairs); one of these two was Camille du Locle, an ambitious young hack-writer who would quite soon be instrumental in the production of *Aida*. *Don Carlos* finally had its première in 1867 and was a moderate success. It was the first Verdi opera to incur the accusation of "Wagnerism"— a criticism which did nothing to alleviate Verdi's sour mood.

Nor did the next two years' events offer much cheer. First, Verdi's aged father died. (It was shortly after this that the Verdis adopted the young daughter of a cousin, whom they raised as their

* *Don Carlo* is the Italian version of *Don Carlos*.

A contemporary cartoon showing
Verdi and the censor arguing over
Un Ballo in Maschera.

(Verdi nelle Immagini)

(Verdi nelle Immagini)

A cartoon by Delfico picturing Verdi rehearsing his singers.

(Verdi nelle Immagini)

Verdi's name was used as an acrostic for Vittorio Emmanuele, Re d'Italia.

(Verdi nelle Immagini)

Verdi presents the plebiscite of Emilia to King Vittorio Emmanuele II in 1859.

own child, and who subsequently became Verdi's sole heir.) Then Antonio Barezzi, Verdi's earliest benefactor and staunchest friend, died—a deep blow to both Verdi and his wife, though they had already nursed Barezzi through a previous stroke. In November 1868, Gioacchino Rossini died in France, where he had lived for many years. When he was in Paris, Verdi often visited Rossini; he had watched Verdi's ascent, sending him letters addressed to "Signor Giuseppe Verdi, Celebrated Composer of Music." At Rossini's death, Verdi proposed a Requiem Mass to his memory, to be written by himself and several of Italy's other leading composers. The purpose of the potpourri that would necessarily result from this scheme was to be commemorative rather than artistic; the Mass would be performed publicly only once, then given to the Archives of the City of Bologna. None of the composers was to be paid for his share of the work, which would be a labor of love. Verdi's own generosity, however, caused him to over-estimate that of other musicians. The project languished and was dropped; a few years later, Verdi composed a complete Requiem incorporating what he had written as his share in the Rossini Mass.

Various matters, including improvements and revisions of some of his earlier operas, kept Verdi busy well into 1869. Toward the end of that year someone (Verdi did not specify who—it was probably Camille du Locle, the *Don Carlos* co-librettist) asked him to write an opera for a "far-distant land." Verdi refused the request, mainly because he could not find a plot which especially interested him. The following spring, when the composer went briefly to Paris, du Locle reopened the subject.

Du Locle was ambitious—his ultimate aim was to become the director of the Opéra-Comique in Paris. If he could persuade the renowned Verdi to present that theater with an original work, it would be a long step forward. For some time du Locle had tried to do this, without success. But when he met the composer in the spring of 1870, du Locle temporarily dropped the question of a new opera for Paris, and concentrated on urging Verdi to accept the commission which had been offered him the previous winter. As events developed, this commission was from the Khedive of Egypt, who wanted the opera to celebrate the opening of a new theater in Cairo which had been built to celebrate the opening of the Suez Canal.* Verdi again refused—perhaps less firmly than before—and returned to Sant'Agata.

Du Locle continued to propose subjects for operatic treatment. Only one of these met with the composer's approval: the brief Egyptian sketch whose striking possibilities were immediately recognized by Verdi. At first, du Locle was vague about the scenario's author. Verdi apparently believed for some time that the story was the work of the Khedive himself, but it presently developed that it had been written by Auguste Mariette (titled Mariette Bey), a famous French Egyptologist.

Du Locle forthwith appeared at Sant'Agata and, under Verdi's surveillance, turned the short plot outline into French prose. Verdi, meanwhile, communicated with Ricordi about a librettist to set the piece into Italian rhyme. Antonio Ghislanzoni, a gifted if eccentric gentleman, was decided on and thus *Aida* was born.

Mariette Bey was consulted on details of Egyptian rites and customs; Verdi closely supervised Ghislanzoni's work, sometimes stating the exact metrical structures he wanted, sometimes even supplying the words the poet was to use. The work proceeded rapidly; it looked as if *Aida* would actually be presented in January 1871, the exact time for which it was scheduled, but the Franco-Prussian War broke out, and the whole affair came to a standstill. Mariette Bey, the technical adviser, was trapped in Paris, as were the extremely elaborate scenery and costumes ordered by the Khedive for the opera. The Khedive worried lest in the interim Verdi would give another opera house the première of *Aida*, which he naturally wanted to reserve for Cairo. Verdi, who would have been technically within the rights of his contract in presenting *Aida* elsewhere, honorably assured the Khedive that the première would be reserved for Cairo. Further, the composer gave a sizable amount of his fee to aid French soldiers wounded during the war. Paris fell and plans for *Aida's* production were resumed. Finally, after lengthy debate over the choice of conductor and performing artists, the opera was presented in Cairo on December 24, 1871.

* The choice of composer for the Khedive's opera seemed to be between Wagner and Gounod if Verdi continued to refuse; but the political situation eliminated Wagner, and before Gounod could be approached, Verdi finally accepted.

The event was preceded by an almost unheard of volume of publicity which has scarcely been matched in the annals of music. Verdi himself refused to go—ostensibly because, as he wrote in a letter, he was afraid the Egyptians would mummify him. Instead, he delegated a trusted student and friend to supervise the staging. Almost every major European newspaper sent critics to Cairo for the première of *Aida*, a fact which considerably irritated Verdi. Time was, said the composer, when an opera could stand or fall on its own merits without a lot of attendant publicity and ballyhoo; now, he added, so many people made so much fuss about a new work that the impact of their noise was greater than the impact of the performance.

Aida was a huge and glittering success, which was shortly repeated in Italy and throughout Europe. Nonetheless, the critics again raised the question of "Wagnerism," and aroused Verdi's resentment so much that he not only derived small pleasure from the opera's triumph, but also disliked having much to do with it for some time.

Verdi was at Sant'Agata in May, 1873, when he heard of the death of Alessandro Manzoni. The composer's regard for this Italian poet and patriot was almost hero-worship; Verdi regarded his only meeting with Manzoni as one of the great events in his life. Though too shaken even to attend Manzoni's funeral, Verdi composed a Requiem Mass in his memory. Despite its sacred text this piece has a definite operatic quality and was enormously successful wherever it was sung. Verdi himself conducted performances of it in Europe's major cities.

During the next several years, Verdi's musical output consisted of some sacred songs, and a revision of *Simon Boccanegra*. The publisher Ricordi and various friends urged Verdi to compose a new work; but the Maestro was tired from his travels and more interested in maintaining privacy and solitude at Sant'Agata than in reaping fresh acclaim. He was in his sixties—too old, he felt, to write anything that could be more than an echo of his earlier vigor. In 1879, Verdi was persuaded into reading a tentative outline of an opera based on Shakespeare's *Othello*. The outline was by Arrigo Boito, who, by this time, had outgrown his youthful impetuosity and was again on good terms with Verdi. Boito knew the various problems of producing an opera; his own *Mefistofele* had recently been an enormous popular failure, though something of a critical success. Above all, he had a genius for turning material into really first-rate libretti. *Otello's* excellence is usually attributed as much to Boito's text as to Verdi's music.

Otello, finally completed in 1886, was the first new opera to come from Verdi in over fourteen years. Verdi had kept the details and descriptions of it a strict secret. He himself directed rehearsals with all his characteristic energy of twenty years before. On the day in February 1887 when *Otello* was finally to be performed at La Scala, the public was almost beside itself with curiosity. Interest mounted to fever pitch; nobody talked about anything else. The opera was received with such enthusiasm that the audience unhitched the horses of Verdi's carriage, and after the performance drew the vehicle by themselves back to his hotel. From a balcony of the hotel, Verdi acknowledged the applause of the crowd. Verdi experienced many emotions; he was deeply moved by the public's obvious warmth and affection for him; he was depressed by the thought that this work, produced in his seventy-third year, would surely be his last; and he was terribly tired from the work and excitement. He wanted sleep, peace, quiet, and privacy. Still, at the reception that followed the performance the old man was heard to say that if he were twenty years younger, nothing would please him more than to compose still another new work—provided he again had Boito to write the libretto.

Verdi returned to Sant'Agata and again devoted himself to maintaining his much desired privacy. He fended off numerous attempts to celebrate a jubilee of his first opera and other offers which threatened him with abhorred publicity. He was saddened by the deaths of other close friends and he considered his career definitely ended. Still, in 1889, the *Falstaff* project began to take shape.

It was hard for Verdi to believe that he, a man nearing eighty, could produce a successful comic opera. He complained that his friends overestimated his good health, and undertook the composition more for his own diversion than with any fixed intent of finishing it. Ricordi and Boito were primarily responsible for encouraging him. Boito's adaptation of *The Merry Wives of Windsor* seemed to Verdi the best lyric-comedy libretto he had ever seen. *Falstaff* was finished in 1893; it was presented at La Scala and was, of course, another triumphant success. The critics found the comedy truly sparkling, though its music was declared a little above the average public taste. Indeed, *Falstaff* has never achieved the popularity of other comic operas such as *Le Nozze di Figaro*, *Il Barbiere di Siviglia*, or *Die Meistersinger*—but it was by Verdi, the Patriarch of Busseto and the Grand Old Man of Italian music. And no matter what individual members of the audience thought of the work, their love and reverence for the Old Maestro outweighed all other considerations.

Falstaff caused fresh waves of acclaim and enthusiasm for Verdi all over Europe. The old man was touched, though he rather brusquely turned down a patent of nobility the Italian government wanted to give him. (He thought it ludicrous.) He also refused a German newspaper's suggestion that he write his memoirs. With pretended consternation at the idea, he said that too many people had been forced to listen for too long to too much of his music without having his prose imposed on them as well.

For the rest of his life, Verdi remained mostly at Sant'Agata. He did travel to Paris in 1894 to supervise the first performance of *Falstaff* in that city; he visited Genoa and one or two other places, but the Busseto countryside attracted him most. Besides, a new project occupied his attention. This was a home for aged musicians which was being built in Milan according to his instructions. Verdi had long cherished this project and had bought the land for it some years before. The Casa di Riposo for retired musicians, sheltering one hundred elderly people, still flourishes today, supported by continuing royalties from Verdi's music.

Giuseppina Strepponi Verdi died in November 1897. She had shared most of Verdi's triumphs and defeats; often she let herself be roused from a sound sleep when Verdi, working into the night, wanted her to hear his latest composition. Her humor and charm, mixed with down-to-earth practicality, had sustained Verdi through bitter moods and black moments. Giuseppina's death was the beginning of the end for the old man, too.

Sant'Agata remained Verdi's home for the four summers left to him. Maria Carrara, the girl cousin he had adopted, was his faithful nurse and companion. Such old friends as remained—Boito, Ricordi—visited him and were welcomed, and he continued to spend the winter months in Genoa. Outwardly still robust and alert, he occasionally complained of failing eyesight and general fatigue and weakness. On January 21, 1901, while dressing, the old man dropped a shirt stud. Too proud to call for help, he tried to retrieve it himself. The effort brought on a stroke; Verdi never recovered consciousness and died six days later.

According to the wishes he had expressed in his will, Verdi was buried in a crypt beside Giuseppina in the aged musicians' home. He had requested a simple ceremony, to take place at dawn or sunset, without music or formalities. Tributes and condolences poured in from the entire world but Verdi's last wish—typical in its dignity and simplicity—was carried out.

Verdi's will was a simple document, written in his own hand. In it he made bequests to his servants and such few relations as still lived. He asked that on the day after his death one thousand lire be distributed among the needy of the village of Sant'Agata. His cousin, Maria Carrara, received about half his property, and the remainder was left entirely to various charities, the major portion going to the Rest Home for Musicians in Milan.

BRIEF BIOGRAPHIES OF OTHER
PRINCIPALS CONCERNED WITH AIDA

Ghislanzoni:

Antonio Ghislanzoni, *Aida*'s librettist, was a rather eccentric gentleman whose life more closely resembles fiction than truth. Born in 1824, Ghislanzoni began his professional career by studying medicine. Finding this unsatisfactory, he turned first to performing on the bass viol, and then, in 1846, to singing. Once, during an appearance on a provincial stage, he recalled an urgent appointment in Milan. Immediately after the performance, he caught a train to that city, without bothering to change from his costume; and, somewhat to the mystification of the Milanese, appeared in their Cathedral Square in the full regalia of a Roman general.

In 1848 Ghislanzoni founded two violently republican journals. The enterprise resulted in his arrest and deportation to Corsica. After his release from prison he returned to singing (he appeared in an 1851 Paris performance of Verdi's *Ernani*); but the loss of his voice forced him to abandon this profession. He returned to Milan as a journalist and critic, and in 1856 published a novel which, while outrageous in both style and content, still shed some interesting light on contemporary theatrical life.

Ghislanzoni had been friendly with Verdi for some time when the composer suggested that he write the *Aida* libretto. Ghislanzoni seems to have accepted the task gleefully, announcing that to save wear and tear on his legs, he would arrive at Sant'Agata borne by a Nubian slave, who would be fed to the dogs upon his arrival. His association with Verdi was a happy one, though Verdi

33

demanded frequent revisions and often dictated to the poet the very words to be used. Ghislanzoni wrote more than sixty libretti —mostly for operas which are completely unknown today. Before his death in 1893, he also helped establish a literary journal (whose contents consisted of ill-disguised political satire), and published numerous other works.

Du Locle:

In 1871, Camille du Locle finally realized one of his ambitions by becoming Director of the Paris Opéra-Comique. Du Locle, the son of a famous French sculptor, was born in 1832 and began his career as a dutiful hackwriter and translator of libretti for the Paris Opéra. He was immensely proud of his share in *Aida*, and continued to insist somewhat futilely that the score's title-page read "*Verses* by Ghislanzoni," rather than "Poem by Ghislanzoni" —since, according to du Locle, the Italian's work consisted only of versifying what he, du Locle, had already written out page by page, and scene by scene.

Du Locle resigned his directorship of the Opéra-Comique in 1877, but continued to write and translate libretti, including several more of Verdi's. In 1887 he was awarded a prize for his work by the French Academy. He eventually retired to Capri, where he died in 1903.

Mariette:

Auguste Ferdinand François Mariette, who wrote the original sketch of *Aida*, was born in Boulogne, France, in 1821. Sent by the government to acquire ancient manuscripts for French museums, Mariette went to Egypt in 1850. There he became interested in archaeology and helped to discover and disinter the Serapeum at Memphis.

Memphis, the ancient capital of Egypt, lay a short distance south of what is now Cairo. Its Serapeum—i.e. Temple of Serapis —was the tomb of the various sacred bulls (named Apis) that were worshipped as living incarnations of the Egyptian god Osiris. The Serapeum differed from other Egyptian temples in having corridors which slanted down from the main structure into huge underground chambers carved out of the rock on which the temple stood. Somewhere in his researches, Mariette seems to

Antonio Ghislanzoni, the poet who was Verdi's librettist for *Aida*.

(Verdi nelle Immagini)

Verdi trying to come up with a new idea. A caricature by Count Melchiorre Delfico. Just before work started on *Aida* some critics thought Verdi's source of inspiration had been exhausted.

Giuseppina Strepponi Verdi, circa 1871.

Giuseppe Verdi, circa 1871. At the time of the première of *Aida*, Verdi was 58 years old.

A page of the Dies Irae section of the *Requiem* for Manzoni, first performed in 1874.

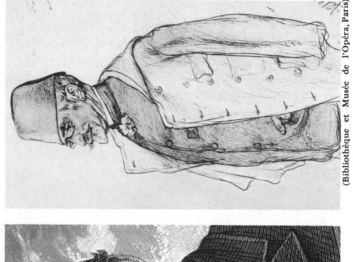

Camille du Locle, who wrote the plot of *Aida* in French prose from Mariette Bey's sketch.

Ismael Pasha, Khedive of Egypt, who commissioned the opera *Aida*.

Auguste Ferdinand François Mariette, French Egyptologist who wrote the original sketch for *Aida*.

have found a vague reference to an ancient Egyptian practice of live entombment; and this, plus the Serapeum's peculiar construction, apparently suggested to him the story outline which became the plot of *Aida*. At any rate, he proposed to Ismael Pasha, Egypt's European-educated Khedive, that an original opera (perhaps based on the little romance he had written) be written expressly to inaugurate Cairo's new opera house.

Mariette's archaeological discoveries resulted in his being appointed Assistant Director of Egyptology at the Louvre. Egypt awarded him the titles of "Bey" and "Pasha." After the Franco-Prussian War, Mariette settled permanently in Egypt. He became Curator of Ancient Monuments to the Khedive (later the ex-Khedive), and founded an important museum at Boulaq, where he died in 1881.

SOME NOTES ON EARLY
PERFORMANCES

Aida's long awaited Cairo première was probably the most publicized event of its sort in operatic history. Important newspapers and magazines from all over Europe sent reporters to cover the event; music critics who attended went home and wrote memoirs in which they described the première and their impressions of it.

By December 1871, the plush, ornate Cairo opera house had been in use for three years. Paying fantastic salaries, Ismael Pasha, the Khedive of Egypt, had lured first-rate talent to his theater, and provided his singers with the most elaborate décor money could buy. The costumes and scenery for *Aida* were ordered from Paris; Amneris wore a coronet of real gold, and Radames was armed with solid silver weapons. The whole effect was so overwhelming that until recently, opera houses presenting *Aida* have copied costumes, props, and scenery of the original performance as closely as possible, with few changes.

As of December 16, 1871, the date for the première was still in doubt; the stagehands were having trouble with the opera's complex machinery. Seats for the performance had been sold out for over a week, and daily full-length rehearsals had been in progress even longer. Mariette Bey was in constant attendance to answer questions about the authenticity of the background and actions. At last it was announced that the final dress-rehearsal of *Aida* would take place on December 23, and the première the next evening; the Khedive was planning to leave town, and the affair could not be postponed any longer.

The dress-rehearsal began at 7 P.M. on Saturday the 23rd, and lasted until after 3 the next morning. Although the music went very smoothly, the stage crew was still having trouble, and the *mise en scène* was cast into total darkness at sundry inopportune moments. Following the nineteenth-century custom, the dress-rehearsal was almost exactly like opening night in the splendor of the occasion and the glittering celebrities who attended. The Khedive, who was present, was so pleased with it all that he immediately ordered a congratulatory telegram sent to Verdi in his name.

The next night the theater was packed long before curtain-time. The audience was almost as colorful as the performance: members of Cairo's many religious and ethnical groups wore their own bright-hued garments and headgear. The Khedive entered during the middle of the prelude and was wildly applauded. Then everybody settled down to concentrate on the opera, and this was wildly applauded too, especially the solo arias and ballets, which were *very* wildly applauded. An astonished and delighted audience went home from the Cairo opera house that night.

All the journalists hurried off reports to their publications. Filippo Filippi, the leading Italian music critic, declared himself confirmed in his previous opinion, that this would be the great Maestro Verdi's best work to date. Filippi further added that at last he was sure Verdi's genius was on a par with Wagner's (a highly doubtful compliment, so far as Verdi and his admirers were concerned).

The French critic Reyer, a composer of operas in his own right, lamented the fact that Ghislanzoni's name rather than du Locle's appeared on the program. This was his chief complaint; as for the opera, he had always thought Verdi's work mediocre, but he found *Aida* very interesting and remarkable—in fact, he was sure it would be appreciated as much in France as in Italy. Quite a compliment from a composer for the Paris Opéra and a confirmed Wagnerian, to boot.

The English magazine *The Athenaeum*, had never been very friendly toward Verdi. (In fact, *The Athenaeum* expressed hostility toward nearly all the leading composers of the day.) Their correspondent decided that *Aida* was better to look at than to listen to, although he was sure that when *Aida* came to England, the scenery from previous operatic war-horses would just have to be good enough, since there was little danger of any European producer's spending as much on staging as the Khedive had. The British critic deplored *Aida*'s dearth of pretty music and the "pale Wagnerism" of Verdi's style. The plot also made him unhappy: ". . . Awful catastrophes are Signor Verdi's special attributes." Finally, mused the critic, "As we have banished the Romans and Greeks from the lyric stage, perhaps the Egyptians and Ethiopians may become our operatic lions." He was quite right, of course.

The European première of *Aida* took place a few weeks later, at La Scala. Verdi himself rehearsed the principals, both at the piano and on the conductor's podium. With energy that would have done credit to a much younger man, he made his customary demands for perfection. Teresa Stolz and Maria Waldmann, whose portrayal of *Aida*'s female leads remain perhaps unequalled, met Verdi's standards; but the tenor, one Fancelli, sorely tried the composer's patience. Fancelli had an excellent voice, but little training in how to use it. Verdi's demands struck the singer as ridiculously exorbitant; why, he complained to a friend, this Maestro expected him not only to read the music as it was written, but also to follow his tempo and the dynamics and, worst of all, to memorize the words! The La Scala performance assured almost everyone that *Aida* was a real masterpiece, designed for universal fame and affection.

Music critics and savants are often remembered for their ability to recognize a work of genius long before it receives public acclaim. Prospero Bertani, however, achieved a sort of unique immortality by strenuously dissenting with both critical and public opinion, and making his dissent known. In May 1872, Signor Bertani decided to attend a performance of *Aida* in the city of Parma and see what all the fuss was about. He didn't like the opera, but was willing to give it another chance; so he again went to Parma (and again subjected himself to a dreadful dinner at the railroad station en route), attended the opera a second time, and once more found it, in his opinion, completely worthless.

Signor Bertani was economically dependent on his family and he felt terrible about having wasted so much of their money on these two performances of *Aida*, and the contingent expenses they entailed. He debated with his conscience for a while, and finally

Sophie Cruvelli, a leading soprano in the 1850's.

Teresa Stolz, Aida in the European première, La Scala, 1872.

(Verdi nelle Immagini)   *(Verdi nelle Immagini)*

Maria Waldmann, Amneris in the European première of *Aida*.   Antonietta Pozzoni Anastasi, Aida in the world première at Cairo, 1871.

Interior of the Cairo Opera House, scene of the world première of *Aida*, December 24, 1871.

decided to lay his problem before the man who was ultimately responsible for its existence: Verdi. Signor Bertani therefore wrote Verdi a plaintive letter explaining his dilemma, and enclosed a bill for his expenses on the two journeys to Parma.

Verdi acknowledged Bertani's letter and bill with grave courtesy. Unwilling to have the young man haunted any longer by the memory of his extravagances, the composer paid the bill (deducting from it only the price of the two horrible railway-station dinners, since he felt Bertani could as easily have eaten at home). One condition was attached to the payment: the young man must sign a receipt promising never again to attend a new Verdi opera. It is probably the only time in the entire history of music that such a contract was made.

New Yorkers, to their great pride, were able to see *Aida* in their city before the opera reached either London or Paris. On November 26, 1873, *Aida* was given at the New York Academy of Music with a first-rate cast. In the next day's papers, critics liked it, though they were of the opinion that most of the numbers were too subtle and not tuneful enough ever to be very popular. *The New York Times* called it ". . . grand lyrical drama, not likely, perhaps, to rouse the masses to tumultuous . . . . enthusiasm," although the previous night's audience had certainly applauded loudly enough, especially at the appearance of a full brass band on stage during the Triumphal Scene. The *Times* reviewer sagely observed that the aria "Celeste Aida" ". . . should be sighed rather than sung"—a comment which coincided with Verdi's own opinion of the matter, although most tenors since then have demonstrated ringing exception to this view.

In 1876 *Aida* reached London's Covent Garden. The incomparable Adelina Patti sang the title role, swathed in what looked something like a copy of Catherine the Great's coronation robes. Patti's voice was actually a bit too light for such a dramatic role; but Patti was Patti, and would have been received with enthusiasm if she had appeared in a feather bonnet and yelled Apache warchants. Still, *Aida* was not wholly successful; London that season was intensely absorbed by Wagner, and for some time the Verdi opera was considered something to be looked at rather than listened to.

Though Americans recognized *Aida's* musical merits—whether

or not these provoked the question of "Wagnerism"—the opera continued for years to be thought of primarily as a visual spectacle. Colonel James Mapleson, a famous impresario, presented *Aida* at the Chicago Opera Festival of 1885, and probably established some sort of record for creating the most densely crowded stage in theatrical history. A mob of 2,000 milled around in the wings, waiting for its cues; as a result, the leading soprano (Patti) needed police assistance to get from her dressing-room to the stage. The crowd of extras for the Triumphal Scene included "Five hundred supernumaries with blackened faces, in Oriental garb" (Ethiopian captives, presumably), and six hundred members of the Illinois State Militia, divided into companies of twelve, all marching with lovely precision.

On November 12, 1886, *Aida* was finally performed by the Metropolitan Opera Company of New York—in German. The cast was headed by Frau Herbert-Förster, whose husband, Victor Herbert, was just beginning a promising musical career by playing 'cello in the Met's orchestra. The artists sang earnestly, laboriously, and Germanically. The staging was brilliant, and the performers got curtain calls, but a melancholy *Times* reviewer reflected in the following morning's paper that, really, ". . . different (performers) must be had if Italian opera . . . . is to be sung with German words at the Metropolitan."

In Europe, *Aida*'s popularity continued to grow; but years more passed before it really became an American favorite. That it did become an unrivaled favorite was largely due to the advent of some really exceptional singers who became identified with the opera. There had long been a few outstanding voices that could handle one or another of the parts; about 1900, though, *Aida* began to be performed by those all-star casts whose names still cause opera fans to gasp.

In 1903 a chubby Neapolitan tenor sang the part of Radames for his second operatic appearance in New York. His name was Caruso, and his singing caused such a stir that he and *Aida* were chosen to open the Met's next season. Since then, *Aida* has been the Metropolitan's opening night work more often than any other opera, most recently in 1951. It leads the Met repertory in the number of times it has been performed (well over four hundred—Puccini's *La Bohème* is the runner-up).

Aida, starring Caruso and the soprano Emmy Destinn, again opened the Met in November 1908. This occasion also marked Arturo Toscanini's debut as a conductor in the opera house. Although it has been generally conceded that ". . . the performance . . . does not much matter . . . on opening night," Toscanini won high praise. He could elicit first-rate work from singers as well as orchestra—and it was this performance which fully brought home to the Metropolitan's management what a priceless asset they had found in Caruso.

Aida, now hailed as "the best opera created in Italy," was Caruso's medium on two more opening nights of his Metropolitan Opera career. Hollywood, too, saw its dramatic possibilities. In 1911 a silent film version of the opera was made and, surprisingly enough, followed the original plot quite closely. After that, the idea apparently frightened movie studios for more than forty years, until an Italian film version of *Aida* was released. This featured the voice of Renata Tebaldi and the presence of Sophia Loren in the title role. Even some Broadway producers decided in 1952 that *Aida* might contain a thing or two for them, especially if retitled *My Darlin' Aida*. Prehistoric Egypt was not deemed good box-office appeal, so the locale was shifted to a Tennessee plantation, just before the Civil War. Radames became Ray, a gallant Southern officer.

Aida and her father were Northerners, of course.

PLOT SUMMARY

ACT ONE, SCENE ONE

Characters in order of appearance:
Ramphis and Radames; Amneris; Aida; King; Messenger; Ministers,
Priests, Soldiers, etc.

An orchestral prelude begins this act. The curtain rises on a hall of the Egyptian King's palace in Memphis. Rows of shrubbery, statues, and columns encircle the hall; between them, in the distance, can be seen the Pyramids, temples, etc.

As the opera begins, the priest Ramphis and the soldier Radames are discussing Ethiopia's anticipated invasion of Egypt. Ramphis tells the young soldier that the gods have named the supreme commander of the Egyptian forces; and he, Ramphis, is on his way to inform the King of the gods' choice.

Radames, left alone, expresses the devout hope that the leader whom the gods have designated is himself. For Radames has fallen totally in love with Aida, an Ethiopian slave girl owned by Amneris, daughter of Egypt's King. If given command of the Egyptian forces, Radames could demand Aida's hand as his reward for victory. This happy prospect forms the subject of his aria "Celeste Aida" ("Divine Aida").

The princess Amneris enters, surprising Radames in his pleasant soliloquy. Suspiciously, she asks the reason for his happy expression. Dissembling, he replies it is because he hopes to be chosen to lead Egypt's armies. Certain asides from both parties follow: Radames, not overly fond of his sovereign's daughter, wonders if she could possibly have discovered his secret passion for Aida; and Amneris, warmly inclined toward the young warrior, is suddenly assailed by a horrid fear that he loves someone else. When the slave girl Aida enters, the soldier's agitation is noticed by Amneris, whose suspicions are thus given a focus.

Amneris, however, is all sweetness and light toward her slave. The latter has heard rumors of the Ethiopian invasion, and this, she says, is the cause of *her* unhappiness—since Ethiopia is her homeland. A sort of trio follows, in which each character privately elaborates his own thoughts and fears. Amneris expresses jealousy and contempt for Aida; Aida admits that she is worried not only about her homeland, but also about her love for Radames, which conflicts with her patriotism; and Radames worries lest the princess suspect something between him and Aida.

Now the King enters, followed by Ramphis, other priests, ministers of state, soldiers, etc. The King summons a messenger who confirms the news of the Ethiopian invasion. The crowd reacts with warlike fervor; the King announces that Radames will lead Egypt's forces, and bids the soldier go to the Temple to be consecrated for his task. More praises and war-cries are sung. Aida's confusion increases—should she pray for Radames or for her country? Amneris hands to Radames the Egyptian standards; the priests invoke the help of the gods for the soldier; King and crowd proclaim "War!" All wish Radames a victorious return and depart, leaving Aida alone on stage.

Momentarily fired by the crowd's enthusiasm, Aida has echoed its sentiment that Radames may return a victor. Now, in the aria beginning "Ritorna Vincitor" ("May He Return a Victor"), she catches herself and again bewails her dilemma. She, the daughter of the Ethiopian King (a fact unknown to her Egyptian captors), is in love with her father's archenemy. This love alone has made her servitude in Egypt bearable—how can she deny or forget it? Scene 1 ends as the unhappy Aida pleads for the pity and help of the gods.

ACT ONE, SCENE TWO

Characters in order of their appearance:
Ramphis, Priests, and Priestesses; Radames

Scene 2 takes place inside the Temple of Vulcan at Memphis, a short while later. In the dim light, sacred statues and columns are just discernible. In the center of the stage is a thickly carpeted platform, surmounted by an ornate, gilded altar.

Scene 2 of *Aida* is usually called the "Consecration Scene." It forms a sharp contrast with the emotional scenes that precede and follow. Priestesses invoke the gods and perform a ritual dance. Radames enters; sacred weapons are entrusted to him and the gods' blessing is sought for him in the coming battles. The scene ends as Radames joins Ramphis, priests, and priestesses in their rituals.

ACT TWO, SCENE ONE

Characters in order of their appearance:
Amneris and Slaves; Aida

Some time has passed. The Egyptians, commanded by Radames, have defeated the Ethiopians and are now returning triumphantly with spoils and prisoners. In a lavish and voluptuously furnished room of the palace, Amneris is being prepared by her slaves for the victory banquet.

As the scene opens, the slaves are singing of the victors' return, urging that martial songs be mingled with love songs. Amneris sings of her own particular desires. There is a little ballet of the Moorish slaves. As this ends, Aida enters.

Inviting Aida's confidence, Amneris feigns sympathy for her slave's sorrow at the Ethiopian defeat. She determines, though, to find out once and for all if her suspicions about Aida and Radames are true. She tells the girl that Radames has fallen in battle. Aida's

reaction reveals the truth. Furiously, Amneris admits she lied;
Radames lives, she says, and she, the daughter of the Pharaoh
loves him. How dare Aida—a slave—be her rival for his affection?
Aida pleads for understanding and forgiveness. Amneris swears to
humble her. Aida almost reveals that she, too, is a King's daughter, but catches herself in time. Again seeking divine pity and
assistance in her plight, she follows her proud and angry mistress
to the triumphal scene, while voices from outside chant of the
glorious victory.

ACT TWO, SCENE TWO

Characters in order of appearance:
King, Amneris, Aida; Radames, Ramphis, Amonasro; Priests, Heralds,
Citizens, Soldiers, Slaves, Captives, etc.

A short while later, on a wide, palm-lined avenue in Thebes.
Off to one side is a temple; on the other side, an opulent throne.
The King enters in full state. He is followed by Amneris and her
slaves, including Aida. The King mounts the throne, Amneris
takes her place at his side, and the chorus proclaims the glory of
the sovereign, the country, and the gods. Heralds with long silver
trumpets strut before the King; they are followed by a parade of
the Egyptian army. The priests thank the gods for victory; the
people sing the praises of Radames, the triumphant warrior.

The King summons Radames to receive the laurels of victory
from Amneris's hand, and promises the warrior that no request
will be denied him this day. Radames asks the King to inspect the
prisoners who are brought before the throne. Among the captives
is Amonasro, King of Ethiopia and father of Aida. He wears the
dress of an Ethiopian officer, and only Aida recognizes his true
identity. Greatly surprised, she embraces him, while he entreats
her not to give him away. The Egyptian King calls Amonasro
before him and asks who he is. Amonasro replies that he is an
Ethiopian officer who has fought bravely for his country, and now
seeks mercy for himself and the other prisoners of war. His plea is
echoed by the slaves and captives; at the same time, Ramphis and

the priests urge the king to obey the gods' decree and put to death all the Ethiopians. Meanwhile, Radames observes to himself that Aida's recent sorrows have made her even more beautiful. Amneris, bitterly noticing the amorous glances exchanged by her slave and the victorious soldier, swears revenge.

The various characters and choruses continue to sing these thoughts and desires. Presently, Radames steps forward and asks the King's mercy for the Ethiopian prisoners: Radames believes that Amonasro, their leader, is dead, and without him the enemy is helpless. Ramphis, in his turn, urges that such clemency will only lead to fresh wars and disaster. However, if Radames's plea is granted, at least let the father of Aida be kept as a hostage. The King grants Radames's wish but also heeds Ramphis's advice about holding Amonasro as security against further hostilities. Then the sovereign presents to his warrior the ultimate reward for victory: nothing less than the hand of Amneris, heir to Egypt's throne.

Radames receives his prize with dismay and consternation; Amneris gloats and dares anyone to challenge her satisfaction; Aida tearfully sees her own chances for happiness slip away; Amonasro envisions Ethiopia's revenge; the Egyptian King joins his subjects in a chorus to the glory of their land; Ramphis and his priests praise the gods; the prisoners praise Egypt's mercy, which has restored their freedom. Act Two ends with a huge chorus, as all together the multitude on stage voices these various sentiments.

ACT THREE

Characters in order of appearance:
Ramphis and Amneris; Aida; Amonasro; Radames; Chorus of Priestesses
(off-stage)

Again, some time has elapsed. It is night, just outside the city, near the banks of the Nile. Moonlight illuminates the scene; half hidden by shrubs and rocks in the middle distance stands a temple dedicated to Isis. Inside the temple, priestesses are chanting to the goddess.

A boat glides silently down the river and halts before the temple. Ramphis and Amneris get out, accompanied by a few guards and veiled women. The priest bids Amneris enter the temple and spend the night before her wedding in prayer.

As Ramphis, the princess, and their attendants enter the temple, Aida appears from the shadows. She too is veiled and glances cautiously about her, fearing discovery. She has come to meet Radames here. While waiting for him, she sings the aria "O Patria Mia" ("O My Country"), in which she describes the beautiful homeland she fears never to see again. Suddenly she is startled by the furtive entrance of Amonasro, her father.

Amonasro has been watchful—he knows his daughter loves Radames, and also that her powerful rival in love is the princess Amneris herself. But there is a way out of this dilemma, Amonasro tells Aida: a way which will bring her both happiness with Radames and fulfill her longing to return to the land of her birth. Ethiopia is rearmed and again ready to fight its archenemy, Egypt. Victory for the Ethiopians is assured this time if Amonasro, their leader, can discover the route the Egyptian army will take on its way to battle. Radames commands the Egyptian army—he is in love with Aida—she has his confidence. . . .

Horrified, Aida recoils at the inherent suggestion. Amonasro answers that if she refuses to do as he says, Ethiopia's bloody fate will rest solely on her conscience. Aida begs for his pity and understanding; Amonasro brushes her aside, saying that she is no daughter of his but a mere slave of the Pharaohs. Aida is utterly torn between duty toward her royal father and her country, and her love for Radames. At this point, the latter enters, and Amonasro hides himself.

Radames is overjoyed to see Aida. Everything will be all right, he assures her. But she replies it is too late—if they stay here Amneris's furious vengeance will destroy them all. Only one course remains to them—to flee together to a distant land where, living only for their love, they can forget the rest of the world. This is the duet "Là tra foreste vergine" ("There among the virgin forests"). At first Radames hesitates, but he soon agrees to run away with Aida—revealing to her the very route that the Egyptian army will follow.

Now, Amonasro, having heard what he wanted, steps from his

hiding place, and reveals his true identity to the incredulous and horrified Radames. Aida tries to calm Radames who realizes the enormity of his betrayal; Amonasro urges the pair to flee with him; and, coming out of the temple, Amneris, probably roused from her devotions by the noise outside, shouts "Traitor!" at the hapless soldier.

Amonasro tries to stab Amneris, but is deterred by Radames, who rushes between them. Calling to Aida and her father to flee quickly, the Egyptian leader surrenders to Ramphis, who, with his guards, now appears on the scene.

ACT FOUR, SCENE ONE

Characters in order of appearance:
Amneris; Radames; Ramphis and Priests

A short time has passed, and the scene shifts back once again to a hall in the palace of the Egyptian King. On one side is a doorway leading to the underground courtrooms where the priests are gathered; on the other side is a corridor leading to the cell where Radames is imprisoned. Amneris, woeful and dejected, stands before the courtrooms' entrance.

A brief recitative by Amneris reveals what is happening: the priests are meeting to determine what fate Radames will suffer for his treason. Amneris believes in the soldier's innocence and still loves him with what she herself admits is a mad, destructive passion. She orders the guards to bring Radames to her.

When Radames arrives, the princess tells him his fate hangs in the balance, but she will plead for him at her father's throne. Radames brushes her aside—his intentions were innocent, he says, but he revealed a military secret and is willing to pay the penalty for his indiscretion. To Amneris's entreaty that he clear himself, he replies why bother?—he has nothing left to live for. His Aida is gone—first the princess kept them apart, now she has probably killed the slave girl, and as compensation she offers him the gift of his life!

Amneris denies any guilt of Aida's death. She knows Amonasro was killed, but Aida simply disappeared, and nothing has been heard of her since. If Radames will promise once and for all to forget the girl, she, Amneris, will save him. Radames coldly refuses and says he is quite prepared to die. The spurned Amneris's passion momentarily turns to hatred; she assures the warrior that his death will avenge the many tears she has shed for him. Radames, declaring that he fears nothing so much as her pity for him, is led away, and Amneris collapses weeping, just as the priests slowly file across the stage and Radames is conducted to them. Amneris, repenting her momentary fury, blames herself for casting Radames to his fate.

After a short unaccompanied invocation to the gods, the priests charge Radames with betraying his country's secrets and demand an explanation. He does not reply; they call "Traitor." The accusations and demands for explanation are repeated—but Radames refuses to defend himself and is condemned to die by being entombed alive. Bitterly, Amneris curses the priests' verdict; ignoring her, they solemnly file out and exit, followed by the frantic princess.

ACT FOUR, SCENE TWO

Characters in order of their appearance:
Radames; Aida; Priests and Priestesses; Amneris

A short time has passed since Radames was sentenced. The stage is divided into two horizontal levels. The upper level shows the interior of the Temple of Vulcan at Memphis—glittering, ornate, bathed in light. The lower level is a dark, gloomy vault. Thick pillars support the ceiling; the pillars, in turn, are supported by grotesque statues. Radames is on the stairs leading down into the vault; behind him, two priests shift into place the massive stone which will forever seal the vault.

Radames, resigned to his fate, hopes only that Aida will live happily, without ever learning of his doom. He sees a shadowy form in the vault—it is Aida, who has concealed herself in his tomb, so that she may die with him. Above them, the priests begin to chant slow prayers. Radames makes a desperate effort to dislodge the stone which closes the entrance. He fails, and sadly acknowledges the inevitability of death for himself and Aida. They sing a farewell to life in the duet "O terra addio" ("Farewell, O Earth"). Above them, Amneris, dressed in heavy robes of mourning, enters and flings herself on the stone that seals the vault. The voice of Amneris, pleading for herself and for the soul of Radames, now mingles with the duet from below. Aida dies in Radames's arms, the priests and priestesses resume their chant, and the curtain falls on this, the final scene of the opera.

MUSICAL BACKGROUND

Until the nineteenth century, almost everywhere except in France, the Italian tradition virtually governed the composition and production of operas. Most of the best-known non-Italian opera composers adhered quite closely to the styles, forms, and theories which had been taught by Italian schools for more than two hundred years.

In Italian opera, melody predominated, and the human voice was its prime vehicle. Frequently the words were of secondary importance; operas consisted of a framework of recitatives whose main purpose was to provide a bridge between the "set pieces"— arias and ensembles—which formed the heart of the work, and gave all the singers in turn a chance to display whatever vocal gymnastics they were capable of. The result of this was that an opera often came to a standstill so far as plot and action were concerned, while the singers showed off the flexibility and range of their voices.

Presently, Gioacchino Rossini tired of hearing his music made almost unrecognizable by the acrobatic whims of artists, demanded that henceforth performers sing exactly what the composer had written, neither more nor less. But aside from this revolutionary innovation in matters of performance, the structure and content of Italian opera remained much the same. It became increasingly a popular form of entertainment as well as an intellectual or aristocratic one, and a work's success could depend on how much people in all walks of life liked its melodies.

Italian opera reached its first nineteenth-century peak with Rossini, Donizetti, and Bellini. During this time two other operatic schools had evolved and gained enthusiastic followers. The older was the French school of grand opera, whose works were performed primarily in Paris. This school insisted that opera should be written on lines of classical purity. The words were as important as the music, and only first-rate libretti were deemed worthy of performance. A French opera's visual aspect was almost as significant as its words and music; numerous and lengthy ballets were an integral part of every work put on at the Paris Opéra.

The third operatic school to reach prominence was that of German "music drama." Its leading exponent was Richard Wagner, whose theoretical treatises outnumbered his musical works. Wagner and his disciples held that opera was musical drama, not just a vocal vehicle. Therefore, it should be a perfect blend of quasi-symphonic music and singing, with neither aspect predominating. "Set pieces" should be more or less dispensed with; orchestral experimentation and innovation became an important part of the music. Just as Wagner's influence was beginning to be widely felt, and his theories heatedly discussed, Italian opera reached its second nineteenth-century peak in the works of Giuseppe Verdi.

As first-rate composers went, Verdi all but had the field to himself in Italy. By 1845 Rossini had retired; Donizetti was dying; and Bellini—the one Italian composer who was greatly admired by the other schools, regardless how much his compatriots were condemned—had already died, pitifully young. An Italian scholar of the 1850's estimated that during the first decade of Verdi's career, five hundred operas were written and performed in Italy. Verdi's work outlived them, for his genius brought about the culmination of Italian opera in the first half of the nineteenth century. Having once reached this goal, he surpassed it by advancing and perfecting his style until it reached its ultimate development in *Otello* and *Falstaff*. *Aida* was a major step toward this "ultimate development." Though a grand opera of the most spectacular sort, *Aida* moves swiftly forward with a simplicity of plot and unity of action not common in Verdi's previous work. Essentially a union of the French and Italian operatic traditions, it still conveys an aura of Eastern exoticism, practically unsurpassed in any work.

Verdi did not particularly study ancient Egyptian music before composing *Aida*. He was more concerned with visual authenticity,

(Verdi nelle Immagini)

(Verdi nelle Immagini)

(Verdi nelle Immagini)

Gioacchino Rossini

Vincenzo Bellini

Gaetano Donizetti

Three great operatic composers whose work influenced Verdi.

(Verdi nelle Immagini)

Richard Wagner

(Verdi nelle Immagini)

Charles Gounod

Composers contemporary with Verdi. The choice of composer for the Khedive's opera lay between these two after Verdi's initial refusal.

for which the Egyptologist Mariette Bey was his authority, than with musical. The so-called Near Eastern tonal effects, in the Consecration Scene for instance, are the result of Verdi's ingenious instrumentation, harmonization, and the unusual melodic intervals, rather than any deliberate intent by him to compose "genuine antique" music.

Though *Aida* has its quota of set pieces, Verdi tried to avoid stock Italian opera traditions. *Aida* is outstanding in its variety of musical contrasts which still form a completely integrated whole. These contrasts are not only between scenes, as in Act I, but also within scenes, as in Act III, where the music rapidly shifts from the lyric melodies extolling Ethiopia's beauties to the dark, strident tones in which Amonasro describes his war-torn country, or to the martial trumpet background against which Radames sings of his love for Aida and his intention of demanding her hand after his next victory.

In the Triumphal Scene of Act II, a trick of instrumentation works hand-in-glove with the opera's visual aspect to heighten the excitement. Verdi had ascertained that long silver trumpets really were used in ancient Egypt. The music for the Triumphal Scene's heralds not only is composed for two sets of trumpets differing from one another in key, but the key itself shifts in the middle of the famous march, thus directing an audience's attention to the sounds as well as the sights of the pageantry. *Aida*'s Triumphal March, of course, has also been an invaluable aid to American education. What high school graduation could take place without it?

Finding "leitmotifs"—i.e. musical themes repeated each time certain situations occur or are recalled in an opera—had become a popular occupation in musical circles since the rise of Richard Wagner, whose operas brought the idea of the leitmotif to its full development. Verdi, because he associated particular musical phrases with some of *Aida's* characters, was accused of "Wagnerism" by critics who forgot that Verdi had used such themes in his operas for years, in fact, long before he became acquainted at first hand (about 1865) with Wagner's work.

Aida begins with a short prelude (Verdi had originally written an overture for it, but replaced this with the less common form of operatic introduction). The melody which opens the prelude—

the "Aida theme"—is repeated at Aida's entrances in the first scenes of Acts I and II, and in Act III. Contrasted with the prelude's Aida theme is the haughty, sinister motif of the priests. This also is repeated later, as in the Triumphal Scene of Act II, and in the Judgment Scene of Act IV.

Another prominent musical motif is associated with Amneris and represents the princess's jealousy of Aida. It is an excited, almost frenzied theme, which occurs when Amneris questions Radames in the opera's first scene; it is in the musical background of the trio that follows; and can be heard again in Act III, when Aida describes to Radames her fear of Amneris's revenge.

With all its innovations, some of *Aida*'s music harks straight back to the former Verdi. The refrain "Guerra, guerra e morte allo stranier," which is repeated in the first two acts, is typical in its Verdian forthrightness and vigor. (The Triumphal Scene's chorus "Gloria all'Egitto," incidentally, was at one time used by Egypt as its national anthem.) Even Amneris, the opera's most complex and best-realized character, in Act IV, Scene 1, begs the gods' pity in one of those sobbing soprano refrains which could almost have been lifted bodily from *Il Trovatore*.

"Guerra, guerra e morte allo stranier"—a refrain   69
    begun by the King, and taken up by Radames and
    the Chorus in Act I, Scene 1; repeated in Act II,
    Scenes 1 and 2

guer - ra,— guer - ra e morte allo stranier!

"Ritorna vincitor"—sung by Aida in Act I, Scene 1   71

Ri-tor-na vin-ci - tor!...

"Oh patria mia"—sung by Aida in Act III   114

Oh,   pa-tria mia, mai più, mai più— ti ri-vedrò!

AIDA

Grand Opera in Four Acts
Music by Giuseppe Verdi
Libretto by Antonio Ghislanzoni

AIDA

Major characters and their relationship to one another:

AIDA, daughter of Amonasro, King of Ethiopia,
and slave of Amneris, princess of Egypt.
She is in love with Radames . . . . Soprano

RADAMES, captain of the Egyptian army and
Aida's lover . . . . Tenor

AMNERIS, daughter of the King of Egypt, and
mistress of Aida. She is also in love with
Radames . . . . . . Mezzo-soprano

AMONASRO, father of Aida, and King of Ethiopia   Baritone

RAMPHIS, High Priest of Egypt . . . . . Bass

KING OF EGYPT, father of Amneris . . . . Bass

AN EGYPTIAN MESSENGER . . . . . Tenor

HIGH PRIESTESS OF EGYPT . . . . . Soprano

Priests and priestesses; soldiers; royal attendants; heralds; slaves
to Amneris; Ethiopian captives and slaves; Egyptian citizens, etc.

ACT ONE
Scene One

ACT ONE
Scene One

Egypt, in the days of the Pharaohs.
Memphis; a hall in the palace of the Egyptian king.
RAMPHIS, the priest, and RADAMES, the soldier, are talking.

RAMPHIS: Sì: corre voce che l'Etiope ardisca sfidarci ancora, e del Nilo la valle e Tebe minacciar. Fra breve un messo recherà il ver.

Yes: the rumor goes that the Ethiopians will dare to try again, and menace the Valley of the Nile and Thebes. Shortly, a messenger will bring the truth.

RADAMES: La sacra Iside consultasti?

Have you consulted sacred Isis?

RAMPHIS: Ella ha nomato dell' Egizie falangi il condottier supremo.

She has named the supreme commander of the Egyptian phalanxes.

RADAMES: Oh lui felice!

Oh lucky the man!

Ramphis looks meaningfully at Radames.

RAMPHIS: Giovane e prode è desso. Ora, del Nume reco i decreti al Re.

It is one who is young and gallant. Now, I shall bring the Deity's decrees to the King.

Exit Ramphis.

RADAMES: Se quel guerrier io fossi! se il mio sogno si avverasse! Un esercito di prodi da me guidato . . . e la vittoria . . . e il plauso di Menfi tutta! E a te, mia

If that warrior might be I! If my dream were to become real! An army of gallant men led by me . . . and victory . . . and the praises of all Memphis! And to return, wreathed

dolce Aida, tornar di lauri cinto . . . dirti: Per te ho pugnato, per te ho vinto!

Celeste Aida, forma divina . . . mistico serto di luce e fior, del mio pensiero tu sei regina, tu di mia vita sei lo splendor. Il tuo bel cielo vorrei ridarti, le dolci brezze del patrio suol; un regal serto sul crin posarti, egerti un trono vicino al sol, ah! . . . Celeste Aida, forma divina, mistico raggio di luce e fior, del mio pensiero tu sei regina, tu di mia vita sei lo splendor. Il tuo bel cielo vorrei ridarti, le dolci brezze del patrio suol; un regal serto sul crin posarti, egerti un trono vicino al sol, un trono vicino al sol, un trono vicino al sol. . . .

with laurels, to you, my sweet Aida . . . to say to you: for you I have fought, for you I have conquered!
Heavenly Aida, divine form, mystic wreath of light and flowers, you are the queen of my thoughts, you are the splendor of my life. I would restore to you your beautiful skies, the sweet zephyrs of your native soil; place a regal wreath upon your hair, build a throne for you beside the sun, ah! . . . Heavenly Aida, divine form, mystic beam of light and flowers, you are the queen of my thoughts, you are the splendor of my life. I would restore to you your beautiful sky, the sweet zephyrs of your native soil; place a regal wreath upon your hair, build a throne for you beside the sun, a throne beside the sun, a throne beside the sun. . . .

Enter the Princess Amneris.

AMNERIS: Quale insolita gioia nel tuo sguardo. Di quale nobil fierezza ti balena il volto! Degna d'invidia oh! quanto saria la donna il cui bramato aspetto tanta luce di gaudio in te destasse!

What unusual joy is in your countenance. What noble fieriness brightens your face! Oh! how enviable would be the woman whose presence is so longed-after that it kindles such light of joy in you!

RADAMES: D'un sogno avventuroso si beava il mio cuore. Oggi, la Diva profferse il nome del guerrier che al

My heart was rejoicing in an adventurous dream. Today, the goddess has divulged the name of the warrior who will

campo le schiere Egizie con-
durrà. . . . Ah! s'io fossi a
tal onor prescelto. . . .

lead the Egyptian legions to
the field. . . . Ah! If I were the
one chosen to such honor. . . .

AMNERIS: Nè un altro sogno
mai più gentil . . . più soave
. . . al core ti parlò? Non hai
tu in Menfi desiderii . . .
speranze?

Did never another dream . . .
gentler . . . sweeter . . . speak
to your heart? Have you not
hopes . . . desires in Memphis?

RADAMES: Io? *Quale inchiesta!*
Forse . . . l'arcano amore
scoprì che m'arde in
core. . . .

Aside. I? Such a question! Has
she perhaps uncovered the
secret love that blazes in my
heart?

AMNERIS: Oh! guai se un altro
amore ardesse a lui nel
core!

Aside. Oh! woe if another love
should blaze within his heart!

RADAMES: Della sua schiava il
nome mi lesse nel pensier!

Aside Has she read the name
of her slave in my thoughts!

AMNERIS: Guai se il mio
sguardo penetra questo fatal
mister! Guai se il mio
sguardo penetra questo
fatal mister! Guai se il mio
sguardo penetra questo fatal
mister! oh! guai, oh! guai,
oh! guai!

Aside. Woe if my glance
should penetrate this fatal
secret! Woe if my glance
should penetrate this fatal
secret! Woe if my glance
should penetrate this fatal
secret! Oh! Woe, Oh! Woe,
Oh! Woe!

RADAMES: Forse mi lesse nel
pensier! Forse mi lesse, mi
lesse nel pensier, mi lesse
nel pensier!

Aside. Perhaps she read my
thoughts! Perhaps she read
my thoughts, she read my
thoughts!

Enter Aida.

RADAMES: Dessa!

Seeing her. Herself!

Amneris watches him closely.

AMNERIS: Ei si turba . . . e
quale sguardo rivolse a lei!
Aida! a me rivale forse saria

Aside. He is disturbed . . . and
such a look he gave her! Aida!
Could that one perhaps be

costei? Vieni, o diletta, appressati . . . schiava non sei nè ancella qui dove in dolce fascino io ti chiamai sorella. . . . Piangi? Delle tue lacrime svela il segreto, svela il segreto a me.

my rival? *To Aida.* Come, oh dear girl, come near . . . here, where in sweet attraction I did call you sister, you are neither slave nor handmaiden . . . You weep? Reveal the secret of your tears to me, reveal the secret to me.

AIDA: Ohimè! di guerra fremere l'atroce grido io sento. . . . Per l'infelice patria, per me . . . per voi pavento.

Alas! I hear the terrible shout of war raging . . . I am afraid for my unhappy homeland, for myself . . . for you.

AMNERIS: Favelli il ver? nè s'agita più grave cura in te?

Do you reveal the truth? and no other, more serious care disturbs you?

She continues to watch Aida closely.

Trema! O rea schiava!

Aside. Tremble! Oh guilty slave!

Radames looks at Amneris.

RADAMES: Nel volto a lei balena lo sdegno ed il sospetto. . . .

Aside. Indignation and suspicion flash in her face . . .

AMNERIS: Ah, trema, rea schiava, trema, ch'io nel tuo cor discenda!

Aside. Ah, tremble, guilty slave, tremble that I may enter into your heart!

RADAMES: Guai se l'arcano affetto a noi leggesse in core! Guai se leggesse in cor!

Aside. Woe if she did read the secret affection within our hearts! Woe if she did read into my heart!

AMNERIS: Trema che il ver m'apprenda quel pianto e quel rossor!

Aside. Tremble lest that weeping and that blushing teach me the truth!

AIDA: Ah! . . . no, sulla mia patria non geme il cor, il cor soltanto; quello ch'io

Aside. Ah! . . . no, my heart does not lament only my country; what I pour out is verso è pianto, è pianto, pianto, pianto di sventurato amor! ah! . . . e pianto . . . pianto di sventurato amor! pianto di sventurato amor, è pianto di sventurato amor!

weeping, is weeping, weeping for a wretched love! ah! is weeping . . . weeping for a wretched love! weeping for a wretched love, is weeping for a wretched love!

RADAMES: Nel volto a lei balena lo sdegno ed il sospetto . . . Guai se l'arcano affetto, guai se l'arcano affetto a noi leggesse in cor! Guai se l'arcano affetto a noi leggesse, leggesse in cor! Guai se l'arcano affetto, guai se l'arcano affetto a noi leggesse, leggesse in cor! Ah, guai se a noi leggesse in cor! oh, guai se a noi leggesse in cor, oh guai a noi . . . oh guai, guai se a noi leggesse in cor!

Aside. Indignation and suspicion flash in her face. Woe if she did read the secret affection, the secret affection within our hearts! Woe if she did read, did read the secret affection within our hearts! Woe, woe if she did read, did read the secret affection, the secret affection within our hearts! Ah, woe if she did read into our hearts! Oh, woe, woe to us if she did read into our hearts . . . oh woe, woe if she did read into my heart!

AMNERIS: Rea schiava, trema ch'io nel tuo cor discenda . . . trema che il ver, ah trema che il ver m'apprenda, ah trema che il ver m'apprenda quel pianto e quel rossor! Ah trema che il ver, ah trema che il ver m'apprenda quel pianto e quel rossor! Trema che il ver m'apprenda quel pianto, quel pianto e quel rossor, trema o schiava, trema o schiava, ah! trema!

Aside. Guilty slave, tremble that I may enter into your heart! . . . tremble, ah tremble that I may be taught the truth, the truth, ah tremble lest that weeping and blushing teach me the truth! Ah tremble, ah tremble lest that weeping and blushing teach me the truth, the truth! Tremble lest that weeping and blushing teach me the truth, tremble, oh slave, tremble, oh slave, ah, tremble!

There is a flourish of trumpets. The King's bodyguards enter, followed by the King, Ramphis, ministers, priests, army leaders, etc.

KING: Alta cagion v'aduna, o fidi Egizii, al vostro Re d'intorno. Dai confin d'Etiòpia un Messaggiero dianzi giungea. Gravi novelle ei reca . . . Vi piaccia udirlo. Il Messaggier s'avanzi!

A lofty cause gathers you about your King, o faithful Egyptians. A short time ago, a messenger returned from the borders of Ethiopia. He brings solemn news. . . . May it please you to hear him. *Turns to an officer.* Let the Messenger come forward.

Enter Messenger.

MESSENGER: Il sacro suolo dell' Egitto è invaso dai barbari Etiòpi . . . i nostri campi fur devastati, arse le messi . . . e baldi della facil vittoria, i predatori già marciano su Tebe. . . .

Egypt's sacred soil has been invaded by Ethiopian barbarians . . . our fields have been laid waste, the crops burned . . . and bold from easy victory, the plunderers are already marching on Thebes.

RADAMES, KING, RAMPHIS, AND OTHERS: Ed osan tanto!

So much they dare to do!

MESSENGER: Un guerriero indomabile, feroce, li conduce, Amonasro.

Amonasro, a fierce unconquerable soldier, leads them.

RADAMES AND OTHERS: Il Re!

Their King!

AIDA: Mio padre!

Aside. My father!

MESSENGER: Già Tebe è in armi e dalle cento porte sul barbaro invasore proromperà, guerra recando e morte.

Thebes is already in arms, and will burst forth from its hundred gates, bearing war and death to the barbarian invader.

KING: Sì: guerra e morte il nostro grido sia.

Yes: war and death be our cry.

RAMPHIS: Guerra!

War!

PRIESTS: Guerra!

War!

MINISTERS & SOLDIERS: Guerra!

War!

RADAMES, PRIESTS, SOLDIERS, ETC.: Guerra!

War!

RAMPHIS: Guerra!

War!

PRIESTS, SOLDIERS, MINISTERS: Guerra!

War!

SOLDIERS: Guerra!

War!

RADAMES, RAMPHIS, & OTHERS: Guerra! tremenda, inesorata. . . .

War! terrible and unrelenting . . . .

KING: Iside venerata di nostre schiere invitte già designava il condottier supremo: Radames!

To Radames. Adored Isis has already designated the supreme commander of our invincible legions: Radames!

AIDA, AMNERIS, SOLDIERS AND MINISTERS: Radames!

Radames!

RADAMES: Ah! sien grazie ai Numi! Son paghi i voti miei!

Ah! thanks be to the gods! My vows are rewarded!

CHORUS: Radames! Radames! Radames! Radames!

Radames! Radames! Radames! Radames!

AMNERIS: Ei duce! Ei duce!

Aside. He the leader! He the leader!

AIDA: Io tremo, io tremo.

Aside. I tremble, I tremble.

KING: Or, di Vulcano al tempio muovi o guerrier; le sacre armi ti cingi e alla vittoria vola. Su! del Nilo al sacro lido accorrete, Egizii eroi, da ogni cor proromba il grido: guerra e morte, morte allo stranier!

Now, go to the Temple of Vulcan, o warrior; gird yourself in the sacred arms, and fly to victory. Go! flock together at the sacred banks of the Nile, Egyptian heroes, from every heart let the cry break forth: war and death, death to the foreigner!

RAMPHIS: Gloria ai Numi! Ognun rammenti ch'essi reggono gli eventi, che in poter de' Numi solo stan le sorti . . . del guerrier—

Glory to the gods! Let all remember that they rule these events, that the warrior's fate rests solely in the power of the gods—

CHORUS: Su! Del Nilo al sacro lido sien barriera i nostri petti;

Go! Let our breasts form a barrier at the Nile's sacred banks;

RAMPHIS: —ognun rammenti che in poter dei Numi—

—let all remember that in the power of the gods—

KING: Su! su! del Nilo al sacro lido accorrete, Egizii eroi.

Go! Go! Flock together at the sacred banks of the Nile, Egyptian heroes.

CHORUS: Non echeggi che un sol grido: guerra, guerra e morte allo stranier!

Let only one cry resound: war, war and death to the foreigner!

RAMPHIS: —de' Numi solo stan le sorti del guerrier!

—solely with the gods rests the warrior's fate!

KING: Da ogni cor prorompa un grido: guerra e morte allo stranier!

From every heart let one cry break forth: war and death to the foreigner!

AIDA: Per chi piango? per chi piango? per chi prego? qual poter m'avvince a lui! Deggio amarlo . . . ed è costui . . . un nemico, uno stranier!

Aside. For whom do I weep? for whom do I weep? for whom do I pray? Such force binds me to him! I must love him . . . and this very man is . . . an enemy, a foreigner!

RADAMES: Sacro fremito di gloria tutta l'anima m'investe. Su! corriamo alla vittoria! guerra . . . guerra e morte allo stranier.

A sacred thrill of glory pervades all my soul. Go! let us speed to victory! war . . . war and death to the foreigner.

AMNERIS: Di mia man ricevi, o duce, il vessillo glorioso; ti

Receive from my hand, o leader, the glorious standard;

Act 1, Scene 1. Radames commissioned as the leader of the Egyptian forces.

Act 1, Scene 1. Amneris tries to discern whether Aida is her rival, as Radames looks on. Leontyne Price is Aida, Irene Dalis is Amneris, and Jon Vickers is Radames.

Act 1, Scene 2. During the "Consecration Scene," priests and priestesses invoke the gods to aid Radames in the coming battles. The action takes places inside the Temple of Vulcan at Memphis.

sia guida, ti sia luce della gloria sul sentier—

KING: Su! Del Nilo al sacro lido accorrete, Egizii eroi, da ogni cor prorompa un grido: guerra, guerra e morte allo stranier!

RAMPHIS AND BASS PRIESTS: Gloria ai Numi, e ognun rammenti ch'essi reggono gli eventi che in poter de' Numi solo stan le sorti del guerrier!

MINISTERS AND SOLDIERS: Su! del Nilo al sacro lido sien barriera i nostri petti; non echeggi che un sol grido: guerra, guerra e morte allo stranier!

TENOR PRIESTS: Gloria, gloria ai Numi, che in poter de' Numi solo stan le sorti, stan le sorti, le sorti del guerrier!

MESSENGER: Su! corriamo, su! Corriamo alla vittoria! guerra e morte, guerra e morte allo stranier!

AIDA: Per chi piango? per chi prego? per chi piango? Per chi prego?

AMNERIS:—ti sia guida, ti sia guida, ti sia luce, ti sia luce della gloria sul sentier.

may it lead you, may it be the light of glory on your path—

Go! Flock together at the sacred banks of the Nile, Egyptian heroes, let one cry break forth from every heart: war, war and death to the foreigner!

Glory to the gods, and let all remember that they rule these events, that the warrior's fate rests solely in the power of the gods!

Go! let our breasts form a barrier at the Nile's sacred banks; let only one cry resound: war, war and death to the foreigner!

Glory, glory to the gods, solely in the power of the gods rests the fate, rests the fate, the warrior's fate!

Come! Let us run, come! Let us run to victory! War and death, war and death to the foreigner!

Aside. For whom do I weep? for whom do I pray? for whom do I weep? For whom do I pray?

—may it lead you, may it lead you, may it be your light, may it be your light of glory on the path.

RADAMES: Su! corriamo, su! cor-   Come! let us run, come! let
riamo alla vittoria! Guerra,   us run to victory! War, war
guerra e morte allo stranier!   and death to the foreigner!

KING AND RAMPHIS: Guerra!   War!

PRIESTS: Guerra!   War!

MINISTERS AND SOLDIERS (BASS):
Guerra!   War!

MINISTERS & SOLDIERS (TENOR):
Guerra!   War!

AMNERIS, RADAMES, MESSENGER,
KING, RAMPHIS, PRIESTS, SOL-
DIERS AND MINISTERS: Guerra!   War!

KING AND RAMPHIS: Guerra!   War!

PRIESTS: Guerra!   War!

MINISTERS & SOLDIERS (BASS):
Guerra!   War!

MINISTERS & SOLDIERS (TENOR):
Guerra!   War!

AMNERIS, RADAMES, MESSENGER,
KING, RAMPHIS AND CHORUS:
Guerra! guerra! guerra!   War! war! war! death! war!
sterminio! guerra! guerra!   war! death! death to the
sterminio! sterminio all' in-   invader! death to the invader!
vasor! sterminio all' invasor!

AIDA: Deggio amarlo e veggo   *Aside.* Must I love him and
in lui un nemico, uno stran-   see in him, an enemy, a
ier! Deggio amarlo, è un   foreigner! Must I love him,
nemico, uno stranier!   he is an enemy, a foreigner!

KING, RAMPHIS AND PRIESTS:
Guerra!   War!

AMNERIS, RADAMES, MESSENGER,
MINISTERS   AND   SOLDIERS:
Guerra!   War!

KING, RAMPHIS AND PRIESTS:
Guerra!   War!

AMNERIS, RADAMES, MESSENGER,
SOLDIERS,   AND   MINISTERS:
Guerra!   War!

KING, RAMPHIS AND PRIESTS:
Guerra!   War!

AMNERIS, RADAMES, MESSENGER,
SOLDIERS   AND   MINISTERS:
Guerra!   War!

KING, RAMPHIS AND PRIESTS:
Guerra!   War!

AIDA: Ah! ....   Ah! ....

AMNERIS, RADAMES, MESSENGER,
KING,   RAMPHIS,   PRIESTS,
SOLDIERS   AND   MINISTERS:
Guerra!   War!

AMNERIS: Ritorna vincitor!   *To Radames.* May you return
                                 a victor!

ALL: Ritorna vincitor!   May you return a victor!

All march off, leaving Aida alone on stage.

AIDA: Ritorna vincitor! E dal   May he return a victor! And
mio labbro uscì l'empia   the impious word came from
parola! Vincitor del padre   my lips! Victor over my
mio . . . di lui che impugna   father . . . over him who
l'armi per me . . . per rido-   bears arms for me . . . in
narmi una patria, una reg-   order to restore to me a
gia, e il nome illustre che   country, a palace, and the
qui celar m'è forza! Vin-   illustrious name that I am
citor de' miei fratelli . . .   forced to hide here! Victor
ond'io lo vegga, tinto del   over my brothers . . . and I
sangue amato, trionfar nel   will see him, stained with
plauso dell' Egizie coorti! E   beloved blood, triumphing in
dietro il carro, un Re . . .   the praises of Egypt's cohorts.

mio padre . . . di catene avvinto! L'insana parola o Numi sperdete! al seno d'un padre la figlia rendete; struggete, struggete, struggete le squadre dei nostri oppressor! Ah! Sventurata! Che dissi? E l'amor mio? Dunque scordar poss'io questo fervido amore che, oppressa e schiava, come raggio di sol . . . qui mi beava? Imprecherò la morte a Radames . . . a lui ch'amo pur tanto! Ah! non fu in terra mai da più crudeli angoscie un core affranto! I sacri nomi di padre . . . d'amante nè profferir poss'io, nè ricordar . . . Per l'un . . . per l'altro confusa tremante io piangere vorrei . . . vorrei pregar. Ma la mia prece in bestemmia si muta . . . delitto è il pianto a me . . . colpa il sospir . . . in notte cupa la mente è perduta . . . e nell' ansia crudel vorrei morir. Numi, pietà del mio soffrir! Speme non v'ha pel mio dolor . . . Amor fatal, tremendo amor spezzami il cor . . . fammi morir! Numi, pietà del mio soffrir, ah! . . . pietà, Numi, pietà del mio soffrir. . . . Numi, pietà del mio soffrir, pietà, pietà del mio soffrir!

And behind his chariot, a King, my father . . . bound in chains! Oh gods, let the insane words vanish! restore a daughter to her father's breast; destroy, destroy, destroy the forces of our oppressors! Ah! Wretched woman! What did I say? And my love? Can I then forget the fervent love which like a sunbeam . . . has delighted me here, oppressed and enslaved though I am? Shall I pray for death to Radames . . . even to him, whom I love so much! Ah! never on earth was there a heart more burdened by cruel sorrows! I may neither mention nor recall the sacred names of father . . . of lover . . . Confused, trembling, I would weep . . . I would pray . . . for the one . . . for the other. But my prayer is turned to blasphemy . . . weeping is a crime for me . . . a sigh, guilt . . . thought is lost in the dark night . . . and I would die in my cruel sorrow. Gods, pity my suffering! Is there no hope for my sorrow . . . fatal love, boundless love, break my heart . . . make me die! Gods, pity my suffering, ah! . . . gods, pity my suffering . . . gods, pity my suffering, pity, pity my suffering!

ACT ONE
Scene Two

(San Francisco Opera Association. Photo by Robert Lackenbach)

Act 1, Scene 2. The "Consecration Scene." The sacred sword is entrusted to Radames. Roberto Turrini (left) is Radames and Giorgio Tozzi is Ramphis.

ACT ONE

Scene Two

A short while later, in the Temple of Vulcan at Memphis. White-robed priests and priestesses are performing rites.

PRIESTESSES'CHORUS: (Led by Grand Priestess) Possente, possente Fthà, del mondo spirito animator, ah!... noi t'invochiamo!

Mighty, mighty Ptah, life-giving spirit of the world, ah!... we invoke thee!

RAMPHIS AND PRIESTS: Tu che dal nulla hai tratto l'onde, la terra, il ciel, noi t'invochiamo!

Thou who from nothingness hast created the waves, the earth, the sky, we invoke thee!

GRAND PRIESTESS: Immenso, immenso Fthà, del mondo spirto fecondator, ah!... ah!...

Great, great Ptah, fruitful-making spirit of the world, ah!... ah!...

GRAND PRIESTESS & PRIESTESSES: Noi t'invochiamo!

We invoke thee!

RAMPHIS & PRIESTS: Nume che del tuo spirito sei figlio e genitor, noi t'invochiamo!

God who art son and parent of thy spirit, we invoke thee!

GRAND PRIESTESS: Fuoco increato, eterno... onde ebbe luce il sol, ah!... ah!...

Eternal, uncreated fire . . . whence the sun had its light, ah!... ah!...

GRAND PRIESTESS & PRIESTESSES: Noi t'invochiamo!

We invoke thee!

RAMPHIS & PRIESTS: Vita dell'-Universo, mito d'eterno amor, noi t'invochiam!

Life of the Universe, myth of eternal love, we invoke thee!

GRAND PRIESTESS & PRIESTESSES: Immenso Fthà!

Great Ptah!

RAMPHIS & PRIESTS: . . . noi t'invochiam!

. . . we invoke thee!

There is a short ballet, "Sacred Dance of the Priestesses," during which Radames comes in without armor or weapons. He approaches the altar, where a silver veil is put upon his head.

PRIESTESSES: Immenso Fthà!

Great Ptah!

RAMPHIS & PRIESTS: Noi t'invochiam!

We invoke thee!

Ramphis addresses Radames.

RAMPHIS: Mortal, diletto ai Numi, a te fidate son d'Egitto le sorti. Il sacro brando dal Dio temprato, per tua man diventi ai nemici terror, folgore, morte.

Mortal, beloved by the gods, Egypt's fate is entrusted to you. Through your hand, may the sacred sword, tempered by God, bring fear, fire and death to our enemies.

PRIESTS: Il sacro brando dal Dio temprato, per tua man diventi ai nemici terror, folgore, morte.

Through your hand, may the sacred sword, tempered by God, bring fear, fire, and death to our enemies.

Ramphis addresses an image on the altar.

RAMPHIS: Nume, custode e vindice di questa sacra terra, la mano tua distendi sovra, sovra l'Egizio suol.

God, keeper and avenger of this sacred land, extend thy hand over, over this Egyptian soil.

RADAMES: Nume, che Duce ed arbitro sei d'ogni umana guerra, proteggi tu, difendi d'Egitto il sacro, il sacro suol.

God, who art leader and judge of every human war, protect thou, defend thou Egypt's sacred, sacred soil.

RAMPHIS: La mano tua, la mano tua distendi sovra l'egizio, l'egizio suol.

Extend thy hand, thy hand over the Egyptian, the Egyptian soil.

BASS PRIESTS: Nume, custode e vindice di questa sacra terra, Nume, custode e vindice di questa sacra terra, la mano tua distendi sovra, sovra l'egizio suol!

God, keeper and avenger of this sacred land, God, keeper and avenger of this sacred land, extend thy hand over, over the Egyptian soil!

TENOR PRIESTS: Nume, custode e vindice di questa sacra terra, la mano tua, la mano tua distendi sovra l'egizio, sovra l'egizio suol!

God, keeper and avenger of this sacred land, extend thy hand, thy hand over the Egyptian, over the Egyptian soil!

RAMPHIS: Nume, custode ed arbitro di questa sacra terra, la mano tua distendi sovra, sovra l'egizio suol!

God, keeper and judge of this sacred land, extend thy hand over, over the Egyptian soil!

RADAMES: Proteggi tu, proteggi tu, difendi d'Egitto il sacro, il sacro suol!

Protect thou, protect thou, defend thou Egypt's sacred, sacred soil!

As all end on the word "suol," the Grand Priestess begins again:

GRAND PRIESTESS: Possente, possente Fthà, del mondo creator, ah! . . . ah! . . .

Mighty, mighty Ptah, creator of the world, ah! . . . ah! . . .

RADAMES, RAMPHIS & PRIESTS: Possente Fthà, spirito fecondator—

Mighty Ptah, fruitful-making spirit—

RADAMES: —tu che dal nulla hai tratto il mondo, noi t'invochiamo!

—thou who from nothingness hast created the world, we invoke thee!

RAMPHIS: —tu che dal nulla hai tratto il mondo—

—thou who from nothingness hast created the world—

BASS PRIESTS: —tu che dal nulla hai tratto l'onde, la terra, il cielo, noi t'invochiam, noi t'invochiamo!

—thou who from nothingness hast created the waves, the earth, the sky, we invoke thee, we invoke thee!

TENOR PRIESTS: —tu che dal nulla hai tratto l'onde, la terra, il cielo, noi t'invochiamo!

—thou who from nothingness hast created the waves, the earth, the sky, we invoke thee!

RAMPHIS: —tu che dal nulla hai tratto l'onde, la terra, il cielo, noi t'invochiamo!

—thou who from nothingness hast created the waves, the earth, the sky, we invoke thee!

RADAMES. —Noi t'invochiamo!

We invoke thee!

As all end on "noi t'invochiamo," the Grand Priestess begins again:

GRAND PRIESTESS: Possente Fthà!

Mighty Ptah!

RADAMES, RAMPHIS & PRIESTS: Tu che dal nulla hai tratto il mondo, noi t'invochiamo!

Thou who from nothingness hast created the earth, we invoke thee!

GRAND PRIESTESS: Spirito animator,—

Life-giving spirit,—

RADAMES, RAMPHIS & PRIESTS: —noi t'invochiam!

—we invoke thee!

GRAND PRIESTESS: Spirto fecondator,—

Fruitful-making spirit,—

RADAMES, RAMPHIS & PRIESTS: —noi t'invochiam!

—we invoke thee!

GRAND PRIESTESS: —immenso Fthà—

—mighty Ptah—

RADAMES, RAMPHIS & PRIESTS: —noi t'invochiam!

—we invoke thee!

RADAMES & RAMPHIS: —im-   —mighty Ptah! . . . .
  menso Fthà! . . .

PRIESTESS, RADAMES, RAMPHIS
  & PRIESTS. —immenso Fthà!   —mighty Ptah!

End of Act I

ACT TWO
Scene One

(San Francisco Opera Association. Photo by Robert Lackenbach)

Act 2, Scene 1. Amneris feigns sympathy for Aida's sorrow. Renata Tebaldi is Aida and Claramae Turner is Amneris.

(Lyric Opera of Chicago. Photo by Nancy Sorensen)

Act 2, Scene 1. Amneris in her room. Giulietta Simionato in the 1960 production.

ACT TWO
Scene One

A short time later.
A large, lush and lavish room in the palace. AMNERIS is being prepared by her slaves for a triumphal banquet. The slaves are singing as the curtain rises.

2ND SOPRANOS: Chi mai, chi mai fra gl'inni e i plausi erge alla gloria il vol, al par d'un Dio terribile, fulgente al par del sol? Fulgente al par del sol?

Who is it, who is it that flies to glory midst hymns and praises, like a fearsome god, glowing like the sun? Glowing like the sun?

1ST SOPRANOS: Chi mai . . . fra gl'inni e i plausi erge alla gloria il vol, al par d'un Dio terribile, del sol? Fulgente al par del sol?

Who is it that . . . flies to glory midst hymns and praises, like a fearsome god of the sun? Glowing like the sun?

1ST SOPRANOS: Vieni: sul crin ti piovano contesti ai lauri, ai lauri i fior; suonin di gloria i cantici coi cantici d'amor, coi cantici d'amor.

Come, let wreaths of laurels, laurels entwined with flowers be showered on your hair; let songs of glory sound with songs of love, with songs of love.

2ND SOPRANOS: Vieni: sul crin ti piovano contesti ai lauri i fior; suonin di gloria i cantici coi cantici d'amor.

Come: let wreaths of laurels entwined with flowers be showered on your hair; let songs of glory sound with songs of love.

AMNERIS: Ah! vieni, vieni amor mio, m'inebbria, fammi beato il cor, fammi beato il cor.

Ah! come, come my love, enrapture me, make my heart happy, make my heart happy.

2ND SOPRANOS: Or dove son le barbare orde dello stranier? Siccome nebbia sparvero al soffio del guerrier, al soffio del guerrier. Vieni: di gloria il premio raccogli, o vincitor; t'arrise la vittoria, t'arriderà l'amor.

Where are the barbarian hordes of the foreigner now? Like the fog, they scattered at the warrior's breath, at the warrior's breath. Come, o victor: collect the prize of glory; victory did favor you, love will favor you.

1ST SOPRANOS: Or dove son le barbare orde dello stranier? Siccome nebbia sparvero al soffio, al soffio del guerrier. Vieni: di gloria il premio raccogli, o vincitor, raccogli, o vincitor: t'arrise la vittoria, t'arriderà l'amor, t'arriderà l'amor.

Where are the barbarian hordes of the foreigner now? Like the fog, they scattered at his breath, at the warrior's breath. Come, o victor, come, o victor: collect the prize of glory: victory did smile on you, love will smile on you, love will smile on you.

AMNERIS: Ah! vieni, vieni amor mio, ravvivami d'un caro accento ancor, d'un caro accento ancor!

Ah! come, come, my love, cheer me again with one more dear word, with one more dear word!

The Moorish slaves perform a ballet while others continue to dress and prepare Amneris.

1ST SOPRANOS: Vien: sul crin ti piovano contesti ai lauri, ai lauri i fior; suonin di gloria i cantici coi cantici d'amor, coi cantici d'amor . . . d'amor . . . d'amor.

Come, let wreaths of laurel, of laurel entwined with flowers be showered on your hair; let songs of glory sound with songs of love, with songs of love . . . of love . . . of love.

2ND SOPRANOS: Vieni: sul crin ti piovano contesti ai lauri i

Come: let wreaths of laurel entwined with flowers be

fior; suonin di gloria i cantici coi cantici d'amor, coi
cantici d'amor.

AMNERIS: Ah! vieni, vieni
amor mio, m'inebbria, fammi beato il cor, fammi
beato il cor!) Silenzio! Aida
verso noi s'avanza . . . .
Figlia de'vinti, il suo dolor
m'è sacro.

showered on your hair; let
songs of glory sound with
songs of love, with songs of
love.

Ah! come, come my love, enrapture me, make my heart
happy, make my heart happy!
Silence! Aida approaches us
. . . . Daughter of the vanquished, her sorrow is sacred
to me.

At a signal from Amneris, the slaves retire and Aida enters.

AMNERIS: Nel rivederla il
dubbio atroce in me si
desta . . . il mistero fatal si
squarci alfine.

To herself. Seeing her arouses
the hideous doubt within me
again . . . let the fatal secret
be ripped forth, at last.

Amneris feigns great love toward Aida.

Fu la sorte dell'armi a'tuoi
funesta, povera Aida! Il
lutto che ti pesa sul cor teco
divido. Io son l'amica tua
. . . tutto da me tu avrai . . .
vivrai . . . felice!

The outcome of the battle was
fatal for your people, poor
Aida! I share with you the
sorrow that burdens your
heart. I am your friend . . .
you shall have all that is mine
. . . you shall live . . . happily!

AIDA: Felice esser poss'io lungi
dal suol natio . . . qui dove
ignota m'è la sorte del padre
e dei fratelli?

How can I be happy far from
my homeland . . . here, where
the fate of my father and my
brothers is unknown to me?

AMNERIS: Ben ti compiango!
pure hanno un confine i
mali di quaggiù . . . Sanerà
il tempo le angoscie del tuo
core . . . e più che il tempo,
un Dio possente, amore.

How much I sympathize with
you! Yet the hardships of
this world have an end . . . .
Time will heal the sorrows of
your heart . . . and more than
time, a mighty god, Love.

Aida is touched by these words.

AIDA: Amore, amore! Gaudio
tormento, soave ebbrezza,

Aside. Love, love. Joy torment,
sweet intoxication, cruel

ansia crudel . . . ne'tuoi dolori la vita io sento . . . un tuo sorriso mi schiude il ciel, un tuo sorriso mi schiude il ciel . . . ne'tuoi dolori la vita io sento, un tuo sorriso mi schiude il ciel!

anxiety . . . in your pangs I feel life . . . one of your smiles unlocks heaven to me, one of your smiles unlocks heaven to me . . . in your pangs, I feel life, one of your smiles unlocks heaven to me!

AMNERIS: Ah! quel pallore! . . . quel turbamento svelan l'arcana febbre d'amor . . . D'interrogarla quasi ho sgomento . . . divido l'ansie del suo terror.

Aside. Ah! that pallor! . . . that agitation, they reveal the hidden fever of love . . . I am almost afraid to question her . . . I share the anxiety of her fear.

Amneris looks hard at Aida.

AMNERIS: Ebben: qual nuovo fremito t'assal, gentil Aida? I tuoi segreti svelami, all' amor mio, all'amor mio t'affida . . . Tra i forti che pugnarono della tua patria a danno . . . qualcuno . . . un dolce affanno . . . forse a te in cor destò?

Well then: what new trembling assails you, gentle Aida? Reveal your secrets to me, confide in my affection . . . Among the brave who fought against your country. did someone . . . perhaps . . . arouse sweet concern in your heart?

AIDA: Che parli?

What are you saying?

AMNERIS: A tutti barbara non si mostrò la sorte . . . Se in campo il duce impavido cadde trafitto a morte. . . .

Fate was not unkind to everyone . . . if our fearless leader fell, transfixed by death on the battlefield . . .

AIDA: Che mai dicesti! Misera!

Whatever did you say! Woe!

AMNERIS: Sì . . . Radames da' tuoi fu spento. . . .

Yes . . . Radames was killed by your people . . .

AIDA: Misera!

Woe!

AMNERIS: E pianger puoi?

And you can weep?

AIDA: Per sempre io piangerò!

I shall weep forever!

Antonio Scotti as Amonasro

Enrico Caruso as Radames

Enrico Caruso's caricatures of himself and his contemporaries in roles from
Aida. From *Caricatures by Enrico Caruso*, published by "La Follia di New
York," 1922. Courtesy of the publisher.

Adamo Didur as Ramphis

Emmy Destinn as Aida

(Verdi nelle Immagini)

Gianna Pederzini as Amneris   Adelina Patti as Aida

Famous singers of the past in roles from *Aida*.

Emmy Destinn as Aida   Emma Eames as Aida

Giacomo Lauri Volpi as Radames   Louise Homer as Amneris

Famous singers of the past in roles from *Aida*.

Francesco Tamagno as Radames   Enrico Caruso as Radames

(Columbia Artists Management, Inc.
Photo by Sedge LeBlang)

Renata Tebaldi as Aida

(Gran Teatro del Liceo, Barcelona.
Photo by Sedge LeBlang)

Mario del Monaco as Radames

Contemporary artists in roles from *Aida*.

(Gran Teatro del Liceo, Barcelona.
Foto Sáez)

Manuel Ausensi as Amonasro

(Columbia Artists Management, Inc.)

Irene Dalis as Amneris

AMNERIS: Gli Dei t'han vendicata. . . .

The gods have avenged you . . .

AIDA: Avversi sempre a me furo i Numi. . . .

The gods were always against me . . .

Amneris interrupts angrily.

AMNERIS: Trema! in cor ti lessi, tu l'ami. . . .

Tremble! I read in your heart that you love him . . .

AIDA: Io!

I!

AMNERIS: Non mentire! Un detto ancora e il vero saprò . . . Fissami in volto . . . io t'ingannava . . . Radames vive. . . .

Do not lie! One more word and I shall know the truth. . . . Look me in the face . . . I was lying to you. . . . Radames lives. . . .

AIDA: Vive! ah grazie, o Numi!

He lives! Oh, thank you, gods!

AMNERIS: E ancor mentir tu speri? Si . . . tu l'ami . . . ma l'amo anch'io . . . intendi tu? son tua rivale figlia de'Faraoni. . . .

Do you still hope to lie? Yes . . . you love him . . . but I love him, I too. . . . Do you understand? I, the daughter of the Pharaohs, am your rival. . . .

AIDA: Mia rivale! ebben sia pure . . . Anch'io son tal. . . .

My rival! Well, then let it be so . . . I, likewise, am. . . .

She catches herself and falls at Amneris's feet.

Ah! che dissi mai? Pietà! perdono! ah! Pietà ti prenda del mio dolor . . . È vero . . . io l'amo d'immenso amor . . . Tu sei felice . . . tu sei possente . . . io vivo solo per questo amor!

Ah! whatever did I say? Have pity! Forgive me! ah! Take pity on my sorrow. . . . It is true . . . I love him with a boundless love. . . . You are happy. . . . You are powerful. . . . I live only for this love!

AMNERIS: Trema, vil schiava! spezza il tuo core . . . segnar tua morte può quest'amore . . . Del tuo destino arbitra

Tremble, vile slave! break your heart . . . this love can mean your death . . . I am the judge of your fate. In my heart

sono, d'odio e vendetta le furie ho in cor.

I bear the furies of hate and revenge.

AIDA: Tu sei felice . . . tu sei possente. . . .

You are happy. . . . you are powerful. . . .

AMNERIS: Trema, vil schiava!

Tremble, vile slave!

AIDA: —io vivo solo per quest'amor!

I live only for this love!

AMNERIS: Spezza il tuo cor, spezza il tuo cor, trema, vil schiava!

Break your heart, break your heart, tremble, vile slave!

AIDA: Pietà! Pietà ti prenda del mio dolor. . . .

Pity! Take pity on my sorrow. . . .

AMNERIS: —del tuo destino arbitra io son, d'odio e vendetta le furie ho in cor, le furie in cor!

—I am the judge of your fate, in my heart, in my heart I bear the furies, the furies of hate and revenge!

AIDA: —pietà! Pietà ti prenda del mio dolor!

—pity! Take pity on my sorrow!

Martial voices sound from offstage.

VOICES: Su! del Nilo al sacro lido sien barriera i nostri petti; non echeggi che un sol grido: guerra, guerra e morte allo stranier!

Come! let our breasts form a barrier at the Nile's sacred bank; let only one cry resound: war, war and death to the foreigner!

AMNERIS: Alla pompa che s'appresta meco, o schiava, assisterai; tu prostrata nella polvere, io sul trono accanto al Re.

You shall accompany me to the parade that is coming, slave; you, prostrated in the dust, I on the throne beside the King.

AIDA: Ah! Pietà! Che più mi resta? Un deserto è la mia vita; vivi e regna, il tuo furore io tra breve placherò. Quest'amore che t'irrita nella tomba spegnerò.

Ah! pity! What else is left to me? My life is a waste; live and reign, I shall soon calm your rage. I shall extinguish and bury this love that angers you in a tomb.

AMNERIS: Vien . . . mi segui, apprenderai se lottar . . .

Come . . . you shall follow me, you shall learn if you dare. . . .

AIDA: Ah! pietà!

Ah! pity!

AMNERIS: —tu puoi con me, se lottar tu puoi, tu puoi con me—

—to vie with me, if you dare vie with me—

AIDA: Quest'amor. . . .

This love. . . .

AMNERIS: —apprenderai se lottar tu puoi, tu puoi con me, vieni, mi segui—

—you shall learn if you dare, if you dare to vie with me, come, you shall follow me——

AIDA: —nella tomba io spegnerò, pietà! pietà!

—I shall extinguish it in a tomb, pity! pity!

VOICES FROM OFFSTAGE: Guerra e morte, guerra e morte allo stranier!

War and death, war and death to the foreigner!

AMNERIS: —e apprenderai se lottar tu puoi con me.

—and you shall learn if you dare to vie with me.

VOICES: —guerra e morte allo stranier!

—war and death to the foreigner!

AIDA: Numi, pietà del mio martir—speme non v'ha, speme non v'ha pel mio dolor . . . Numi, pietà del mio soffrir, Numi, pietà! pietà! pietà!

Gods, pity my torment— There is no hope, there is no hope for my sorrow. . . . Gods, pity my suffering, Gods, pity! pity! pity!

ACT TWO
Scene Two

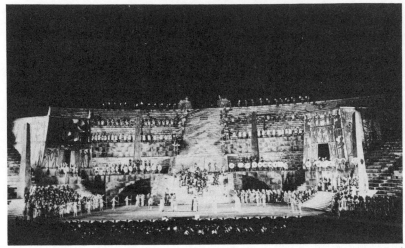

(Musical America)

Two world-famous outdoor productions of *Aida*. Above: The "Triumphal Scene" at the Verona Arena, Italy. Below: The "Triumphal Scene" at the Baths of Caracalla in Rome.

(Musical America)

ACT TWO

Scene Two

"Triumphal Scene"

A short while later, on a wide avenue in Thebes.

*The KING enters in full state and goes to a throne on one side of the stage;
he is followed by army officers, priests, heralds, fan-bearers, etc. Then
come AMNERIS, with AIDA and other slaves. The KING mounts the
throne; AMNERIS goes to his side.*

PEOPLE'S CHORUS: Gloria all'
Egitto, ad Iside che il sacro
suol protegge! Al Re che il
Delta regge, al Re che il
Delta regge inni festosi al-
ziam! Gloria! Gloria!
Gloria!

Glory to Egypt, to Isis who
protects its sacred soil! Let us
raise joyous hymns to the King
who rules the Delta, to the
King who rules the Delta!
Glory! Glory! Glory!

1ST PART OF CHORUS: Gloria al
Re! Gloria, gloria, gloria!
Inni alziam, inni alziam!
Gloria al Re! Inni festosi,
festosi alziam!

Glory to the King! Glory,
glory, glory! Let us raise
hymns! let us raise hymns!
Glory to the King! Let us
raise festive, festive hymns!

2ND PART OF CHORUS: Gloria
al Re! Gloria, gloria, gloria!
Inni alziam, inni alziam!
Gloria al Re, al Re! Inni
festosi alziam!

Glory to the King! Glory,
glory, glory! Let us raise
hymns, let us raise hymns!
Glory to the King, to the
King! Let us raise festive
hymns!

3RD PART OF CHORUS: Gloria, gloria, gloria! Inni alziam, inni alziam! Gloria al Re! Inni festosi alziam!

Glory, glory, glory! Let us raise hymns, let us raise hymns! Glory to the King! Let us raise festive hymns!

4TH PART OF CHORUS: Gloria, gloria, gloria! Inni alziam, inni alziam! Gloria al Re, al Re! Inni festosi alziam!

Glory, glory, glory! Let us raise hymns, let us raise hymns! Glory to the King, to the King! Let us raise festive hymns!

SOPRANOS & CHORUS: S'intrecci il loto al lauro sul crin dei vincitori! Nembo gentil di fiori stenda sull'armi un vel. Danziam, fanciulle egizie, le mistiche carole, come d'intorno al sole danzano gli astri in ciel.

May lotus be interlaced with laurel on the victors' brows. Let a light cloud of flowers spread a veil o'er the weapons. Maidens of Egypt, let us dance the mystic ring dances, as the stars eternally dance around the sun in the sky.

PRIESTS (2ND BASS): Della vittoria agl'arbitri supremi il guardo ergete; grazie agli Dei rendete nel fortunato dì, grazie agli Dei, grazie rendete nel fortunato dì—

Lift your eyes to the supreme arbiters of our victory; render thanks to the gods, thanks to the gods on this fortunate day, render thanks on this fortunate day—

PRIESTS (2ND TENOR): Della vittoria agl'arbitri supremi il guardo ergete, grazie agli Dei rendete nel fortunato dì—

Lift your eyes to the supreme arbiters of our victory, render thanks to the gods on this fortunate day—

PRIESTS (1ST BASS): Della vittoria agl'arbitri supremi il guardo, il guardo ergete; grazie rendete nel fortunato dì—

Lift your eyes, lift your eyes to the supreme arbiters of the victory; render thanks on this fortunate day—

PRIESTS (1ST TENOR): Grazie agli Dei rendete nel fortunato dì—

Render thanks to the gods on this fortunate day—

PRIESTS: —Grazie agli Dei rendete nel fortunato dì.

Render thanks to the gods on this fortunate day.

SOPRANOS: Come d'intorno al sole danzano gli astri in ciel.

As the stars eternally dance around the sun in the sky.

MEN OF CHORUS: Inni festosi alziam al Re, alziamo al Re.

Let us raise, let us raise festive hymns to the King, to the King.

Trumpeters, followed by a body of Egyptian troops, parade before the King. More troops, banners, chariots, and sacred objects enter and cross the stage. They are followed by dancing girls with the spoils of victory.

PEOPLE'S CHORUS: Vieni, o guerriero vindice, vieni a gioir con noi; sul passo degli eroi, sul passo degli eroi i lauri, i fior versiam!

Come, o victorious warrior, come to rejoice with us; let us scatter flowers and laurels on the path of the heroes, on the path of the heroes.

PRIESTS: Agli arbitri supremi il guardo ergete, il guardo ergete, il guardo ergete;

Lift your eyes to the supreme arbiters of the victory, lift your eyes, lift your eyes;

PRIESTS: Grazie agli Dei,—agli Dei rendete nel fortunato dì.

Render thanks to the gods, to the gods on this fortunate day.

PRIESTS (BASS): —nel fortunato dì.

—on this fortunate day.

SOPRANOS: Vieni, o guerrier, vieni a gioir, a gioir con noi, o guerrier, vieni o guerrier, vieni a gioir con noi, vieni, vieni, vieni, o guerrier. . . .

Come, o warrior, come to rejoice, to rejoice with us, o warrior, come, o warrior, come to rejoice with us, come, come, come, o warrior. . . .

PEOPLE'S CHORUS: Gloria, gloria, gloria, gloria al guerrier, gloria al guerrier, vieni, vieni, o guerriero, vieni, o guerrier. . . .

Glory, glory, glory, glory to the warrior, glory to the warrior, come, come, o warrior, come, o warrior. . . .

BASSES: Gloria, gloria, gloria, gloria al guerrier, gloria al

Glory, glory, glory, glory to the warrior, glory to the war-

guerrier, vieni, o guerrier, vieni, o guerriero, vieni, o guerrier. . . .

PRIESTS: Grazie, grazie, grazie, grazie agli Dei, grazie agli Dei rendete, grazie agli Dei. . . .

PEOPLE: —vieni a gioir con noi, sul passo degl'eroi i lauri e i fior versiam. Vieni, o guerriero, vieni a gioir con noi, sul passo degl'eroi i lauri i fior versiam. Gloria, gloria, gloria, gloria all' Egitto, gloria, gloria, all' Egitto, gloria, gloria, gloria, gloria, gloria, gloria!

PRIESTS: —grazie agli Dei, grazie agli Dei, grazie agli Dei rendete, grazie agli Dei rendete, grazie agli Dei rendete, grazie rendete nel fortunato dì, grazie agli Dei, grazie agli Dei, grazie, grazie, grazie rendete agli Dei, grazie, grazie agli Dei!

rior, come, o warrior, come, o warrior, come, o warrior. . . .

Thanks, thanks, thanks, thanks to the gods, render thanks to the gods, thanks to the gods. . . .

—come to rejoice with us, let us scatter laurels and flowers on the path of the heroes. Come, o warrior, come to rejoice with us, let us scatter laurels and flowers on the path of the heroes. Glory, glory, glory, glory to Egypt, glory to Egypt, glory, glory, glory, glory, glory, glory!

—thanks to the gods, thanks to the gods, render thanks to the gods, render thanks to the gods, render thanks to the gods, render thanks on this fortunate day, thanks to the gods, thanks to the gods, thanks, thanks, render thanks to the gods, thanks, thanks to the gods!

The King addresses Radames.

KING: Salvator della patria, io ti saluto. Vieni, e mia figlia di sua man ti porga il serto trionfale.

Savior of the country, I salute you. Come, that my daughter may present to you from her hand the triumphal wreath.

Amneris hands the crown to Radames, who bows very low before her.

KING: Ora a me chiedi quanto più brami. Nulla a te negato sarà in tal dì . . . lo giuro per

Now you may ask of me what you most desire. On this day, nothing will be denied you . . .

la corona mia, pei sacri Numi.	I swear it by my crown, by the sacred gods.

RADAMES: Concedi in pria che innanzi a te sien tratti i prigionier.

First, let it be granted that the prisoners be brought before you.

Enter Ethiopian prisoners, heavily guarded. At their rear, dressed as an Ethiopian officer, comes Amonasro.

RAMPHIS & PRIESTS: Grazie agli Dei, grazie rendete, nel fortunato, nel fortunato dì, grazie, grazie agli Dei.

Thanks to the gods, render thanks, thanks, thanks to the gods on this fortunate, on this fortunate day.

AIDA: Che veggo! Egli! Mio padre!

Whom do I see! Him! My father!

AMNERIS, RADAMES, RAMPHIS, KING, PRIESTS & PEOPLE: Suo padre!

Her father!

AMNERIS: In poter nostro!

In our power!

Aida embraces Amonasro.

AIDA: Tu! prigionier!

You! prisoner!

AMONASRO: Non mi tradir!

Aside to Aida. Do not give me away!

KING: T'appressa . . . Dunque . . . tu sei?

To Amonasro. Come forward . . . .So then . . . you are. . . .

AMONASRO: Suo padre. An- ch'io pugnai . . . vinti noi fummo . . . morte invan cercai.

Her father. I too fought . . . we were conquered . . . in vain I sought death.

Indicates the uniform he wears.

Quest'assisa ch'io vesto vi dica che il mio Re, la mia patria ho difeso; fu la sorte a nostr'armi nemica . . . tornò vano de'forti l'ardir. Al mio

Let this attire that I wear tell you I have defended my king, my country; fate was hostile to our weapons; our heroes' bravery was in vain. Our king

piè nella polve disteso giac-
que il Re da più colpi
trafitto; se l'amor della patria è delitto, siam rei tutti,
siam pronti a morir! Ma tu,
Re, tu signore possente, a
costoro ti volgi clemente
. . . Oggi noi siam percossi
dal fato, ah! Doman voi
potria il fato colpir.

fell at my feet in the dust,
headlong, killed by many
blows; if love of one's country
is a crime, we are all guilty,
we are ready to die! But you,
King, you, powerful lord,
show yourself merciful to these
men . . . today we have been
battered by fate, ah! to-
morrow fate may strike you.

AIDA: Ma tu, Re, tu signore
possente, a costoro ti volgi
clemente . . . Oggi noi siam
percossi dal fato, ah! doman
voi potria il fato colpir.

But you, King, you, powerful
lord, show yourself merciful to
these men . . . today we have
been battered by fate, ah!
tomorrow fate may strike you.

SLAVES & PRISONERS: Sì: dai
Numi percossi noi siamo;
tua pietà, tua clemenza
imploriamo; ah, giammai di
soffrir vi sia dato ciò . . . che
in oggi n'è dato soffrir!

Yes: we have been battered
by the gods; we implore your
mercy, your clemency; ah,
may it never be your lot to
suffer thus . . . as it has befallen us to suffer today!

BASS PRISONER: . . . ciò che n'è
dato soffrir!

. . . thus as it has befallen us to
suffer!

AMONASRO: Ah! doman voi
potria il fato colpir!

Ah! tomorrow fate may strike
you!

RAMPHIS & PRIESTS: Struggi, o
Re . . . queste ciurme feroci,
chiudi il cor alle perfide
voci;

O King, destroy . . . this
vicious pack, close your heart
to their perfidious pleas;

AIDA, SLAVES & PRISONERS:
Pietà!

Mercy!

RAMPHIS & PRIESTS: —fur dai
Numi votati alla morte—

—they were sentenced to
death by the gods—

AIDA, SLAVES & PRISONERS:
Pietà!

Mercy!

RAMPHIS & PRIESTS: —or de'
Numi—

—now let the gods'—

AIDA, SLAVES & PRISONERS:
Pietà!

Mercy!

RAMPHIS & PRIESTS: —si com-
pia il voler!

—wish be fulfilled!

AIDA: Ma tu, o Re, signor
possente, a costoro ti mostra
clemente. . . .

But you, o King, powerful
lord, show yourself merciful to
these men. . . .

AMNERIS: Quali sguardi . . .
quali sguardi . . . sovr'essa
ha rivolti! di qual fiamma
balenano i volti!

Such glances . . . such glances
. . . he casts at her! their faces
glow with such fire!

AMONASRO: Oggi noi siam
percossi dal fato, voi . . .
doman potria il fato colpir.

Today we have been battered
by fate . . . tomorrow fate may
strike you.

RAMPHIS & PRIESTS: A morte!
A morte! A morte! O Re,
struggi, struggi queste ciurme. . . .

To death! To death! To death!
O King, destroy, destroy this
pack. . . .

KING: Or che fausti ne arridon
gli eventi a costoro mos-
triamci clementi. . . .

Now that events have turned
out thus fortunate, let us show
ourselves merciful to these
men. . . .

SLAVES: —tua pietade, tua
clemenza imploriamo, ah,
pietà, pietà,—

—we beseech your pity, your
mercy, ah, mercy, mercy,—

PRISONERS: —tua pietade, tua
clemenza imploriamo, tua
clemenza imploriamo,—

—we beseech your pity, your
mercy, we beseech your
mercy,—

PEOPLE: Sacerdoti, gli sdegni
placate, l'umil prece ascoltate;

Priests, calm your indignation,
hear the humble prayer;

RADAMES: Il dolor che in quel volto favella al mio sguardo la rende più bella;

The sorrow which speaks in that face makes her more beautiful in my eyes;

AMNERIS: —quali sguardi sovr'essa ha rivolti! di quel fiamma balenano i volti!

—such glances he casts at her! their faces glow with such a fire!

AIDA: Tua pietà, imploro.

I beseech your pity.

AMONASRO: Tua pietà, tua clemenza imploriamo—

We beseech your pity, your mercy—

KING: —or che fausti ne arridon gli eventi—

—now that events have turned out thus fortunate—

SLAVES: Pietà!

Mercy!

PRISONERS: Pietà!

Mercy!

RAMPHIS & PRIESTS: —si compisca de'Numi il voler!

—the gods' wish must be fulfilled!

PEOPLE: —sacerdoti, gli sdegni placate,—

—priests, calm your indignation,—

RADAMES: —ogni stilla del pianto adorato nel mio petto ravviva l'amor, ogni stilla del pianto adorato, del pianto adorato nel mio petto, nel mio petto ravviva l'ardor;

—each drop of her beloved tears feeds the love in my breast, each drop of her beloved tears, of her beloved tears, feeds the passion in my breast, in my breast;

AMNERIS: Ed io sola, avvilita, reietta? La vendetta mi rugge nel cor, la vendetta, la vendetta mi rugge nel cor, mi rugge nel core, nel cor.

And I alone, reviled, cast down? Revenge shrieks in my heart, revenge, revenge shrieks in my heart, shrieks in my heart, in my heart.

AMONASRO: —tua pietà, tua clemenza imploriamo, tua clemenza imploriam, tua

We beseech your pity, your mercy, we beseech your mercy, we beseech your mercy, we clemenza imploriam, imploriamo, tua pietade, tua clemenza imploriam.

beseech your pity, we beseech your mercy.

KING: —a costoro mostriamci clementi: la pietà sale ai Numi gradita e rafferma, e rafferma il poter, il poter.

—let us show ourselves merciful to these men: pity rises welcome to the gods, is and reaffirms, and reaffirms power, power.

SLAVES: —ah, pietà! pietà! pietà! Tua pietade, tua clemenza invochiamo, invochiam.

—ah, pity! pity! pity! We beseech, we beseech your pity, your mercy.

PEOPLE: —l'umil prece de' vinti ascoltate; —sacerdoti, gli sdegni placate, pietà!

—hear the humble prayer of the vanquished; —priests, calm your indignation, pity!

AIDA: —oggi noi siam percossi, doman voi potria, potria il fato colpir.

—today we have been battered, tomorrow fate may, may strike you.

PRISONERS: —pietà, tua clemenza imploriam, tua clemenza imploriam, tua pietade, tua clemenza invochiam, invochiam.

—pity, we beseech your mercy, we beseech your mercy we beseech, we beseech your pity, your mercy.

RAMPHIS & PRIESTS: —struggi, o Re, queste ciurme, queste ciurme feroci, struggi, struggi; fur . . . dai Numi votati, fur votati alla morte, si compisca de'Numi, de' Numi il voler!

—o King, destroy, destroy, destroy this pack, this ferocious pack; they were . . . sentenced by the gods, they were sentenced to death, let the gods', the gods' wish be fulfilled!

AIDA: Ma tu, o Re, tu signore possente a costoro ti mostra clemente . . . oggi noi siam percossi dal fato, ah, doman voi potria il fato colpir,

But you, O King, you powerful lord, show yourself merciful to these men . . . today we have been battered by fate, ah, tomorrow fate may strike you,

doman voi, doman voi il fato potria . . . doman voi . . . potria colpir, doman voi potria il fato, doman voi potria colpir . . . voi potria colpir. . . .

tomorrow you, tomorrow fate may strike you . . . tomorrow fate may strike you, tomorrow fate may strike you, tomorrow it may strike you . . . it may strike you. . . .

RADAMES: Il dolor, il dolor la rende più bella; ogni stilla, ogni stilla del pianto adorato nel mio petto, nel mio petto ravviva l'ardor, nel mio petto, nel mio petto, ogni stilla del suo pianto nel mio petto ravviva l'ardor, l'ardor.

Her sorrow, her sorrow makes her more lovely; every drop, every drop of her beloved tears feeds the passion in my breast, in my breast, in my breast, in my breast, every drop of her tears feeds the passion in my breast.

AMONASRO: Ma tu, o Re, tu signore possente, a costoro ti mostra clemente . . . oggi noi siam percossi dal fato, ah doman voi potria il fato colpir, oggi noi, oggi noi siam percossi dal fato, voi doman il fato potria colpir, doman voi potria il fato, doman voi potria colpire, doman voi potria colpir, potria colpir.

But you, O King, you powerful lord, show yourself merciful to these men . . . today we have been battered by fate, ah, tomorrow fate may strike you, today we, today we have been battered by fate, tomorrow fate may strike you, tomorrow fate may, tomorrow it may strike you, tomorrow it may strike you, tomorrow it may strike you, it may strike.

KING: La pietà, la pietà, la pietà, la pietà sale ai Numi gradita e rafferma de'prenci il poter, ai Numi sale gradita e rafferma il poter, rafferma il poter.

Mercy, mercy, mercy, mercy rises welcome to the gods, and reaffirms the power of princes, rises welcome to the gods, and reaffirms the power, reaffirms power.

SLAVES: Sì, dai Numi percossi noi siamo, tua pietà, tua clemenza imploriamo: ah! giammai di soffrir vi sia

Yes, we have been battered by the gods, we beseech your pity your mercy: ah! may it never be your lot to suffer thus as it

Act 2, Scene 2. Amonasro tells Aida not to betray his identity. Robert Weede is Amonasro and Leontyne Price is Aida.

Act 2, Scene 2. Just before the presentation of the victory laurels. Left to right: Aida, Amneris, Ramphis, King of Egypt, Radames.

(Lyric Opera of Chicago. Photo by Nancy Sorensen)

Act 2, Scene 2. Aida bears the laurel wreath which Amneris is to present to Radames. Leontyne Price is Aida and Giulietta Simionato is Amneris in this 1960 performance.

(Museum of the Bolshoi Theater, Moscow)

Act 2, Scene 2. Amneris presents the laurels of victory to Radames, as Aida serves her and the King of Egypt looks on. From the 1951 performance.

Act 2, Scene 2. Finale of the "Triumphal Scene." Left to right: Margherita Roberti as Aida, Robert Merrill as Amonasro, Carlo Bergonzi as Radames, Franco Ventriglia as the King, Giulietta Simionato as Amneris, and Ferruccio Mazzoli as Ramphis.

Act 2, Scene 2. Amonasro in chains before the King of Egypt. Aida, who has recognized him, stands nearby. From a 1947 performance.

Act 2, Scene 2. Ballet sequence from the "Triumphal Scene."

dato ciò che in oggi n'è dato soffrir! Ah giammai, ah giammai di soffrir vi sia dato, ciò che in oggi, ciò che in oggi n'è dato soffrir! Ah, tua clemenza imploriamo, imploriam, imploriam.

PRISONERS: Sì, dai Numi percossi noi siamo, tua pietà, tua clemenza imploriamo; ah! giammai di soffrir vi sia dato ciò che n'è dato soffrir! Ah giammai, ah giammai di soffrir vi sia dato ciò che in oggi, ciò che in oggi n'è dato soffrir! Ah, tua clemenza imploriamo, imploriam, imploriam.

PEOPLE: Re possente, Re possente, e tu, o Re, tu, o Re, tu possente, tu forte, a clemenza, a clemenza dischiudi il pensier, a clemenza dischiudi il pensier, o Re possente, Re.

RAMPHIS & BASS PRIESTS: Struggi, o Re, queste ciurme, queste ciurme feroci, fur dai Numi votati, fur votati alla morte, si compisca de'Numi, si compisca de' Numi il voler! Struggi, o Re . . . struggi, o Re . . . queste ciurme, fur dai Numi votati alla morte, si compisca de'Numi il voler! fur dai Numi, dai Numi votati

has befallen us to suffer today! Ah never, ah never may it be your lot to suffer thus as it has today befallen us, thus as it has today befallen us to suffer! Ah, we beseech, we beseech, we beseech your mercy.

Yes, we have been battered by the gods, we beseech your pity, your mercy: ah! may it never be your lot to suffer thus as it has befallen us to suffer! Ah never, ah never may it be your lot to suffer thus as today, thus as today it has befallen us to suffer! Ah, we beseech, we beseech your mercy.

Mighty King, mighty King, and you, o King, you, o King you mighty one, you strong one, open your thoughts to mercy, open your thoughts to mercy, o powerful King, King.

O King, destroy this pack, this ferocious pack, they were sentenced to death by the gods, they were sentenced to death, the gods be obeyed, let the gods' wish be fulfilled. O King, destroy . . . o King, destroy . . . this pack, they were sentenced to death by the gods, let the gods' wish be fulfilled! they were sentenced to death, they were sentenced

alla morte, fur votati alla morte, si compisca de' Numi il voler, de'Numi il voler!

to death by the gods, by the gods, let the Gods' wish, the Gods' wish be fulfilled!

AMNERIS: Ed io sola, avvilita, avvilita, reietta? . . . la vendetta mi rugge nel cor . . . ed io sola, avvilita, avvilita, reietta? . . . la vendetta, la vendetta rugge nel cor, la vendetta, la vendetta, la vendetta rugge, rugge in cor, rugge in cor, in cor.

And I am alone, reviled, reviled, cast down? . . . revenge shrieks in my heart . . . and I alone, reviled, reviled, cast down? . . . revenge, revenge shrieks in my heart, revenge, revenge, revenge shrieks, shrieks in my heart, shrieks in my heart, in my heart.

TENOR PRIESTS: Struggi, o Re, queste ciurme, queste ciurme feroci, fur dai Numi votati, fur votati alla morte, si compisca de' Numi il voler! struggi, o Re . . . struggi, o Re . . . queste ciurme, fur dai Numi votati alla morte, si compisca de' Numi il voler! fur dai Numi, dai Numi votati alla morte, fur votati alla morte, si compisca de' Numi il voler, de'Numi il voler.

O King, destroy this pack, this ferocious pack, they were sentenced by the gods, they were sentenced to death, let the gods' wish be fulfilled! O King, destroy . . . o King, destroy . . . this pack, they were sentenced to death by the gods, let the gods' wish be fulfilled! They were sentenced to death, they were sentenced to death by the gods, let the gods' wish be fulfilled.

RADAMES: O Re: pei sacri Numi, per lo splendor della tua corona, compier giurasti il voto mio. . . .

O King: by the sacred gods, by the splendor of your crown you swore to fulfill my wishes. . . .

KING: Giurai.

I swore it.

RADAMES: Ebbene: a te pei prigionieri Etiopi vita domando e libertà.

Well then: I ask of you life and freedom for the Ethiopian prisoners.

AMNERIS: Per tutti!

Aside. For all of them!

PRIESTS: Morte ai nemici della patria!

Death to our country's enemies!

PEOPLE: Grazia per gl'infelici!

Mercy for the unhappy ones!

RAMPHIS: Ascolta, o Re. Tu pure, giovine eroe, saggio consiglio ascolta: son nemici e prodi sono ... la vendetta hanno nel cor, fatti audaci dal perdono correranno all'armi ancor!

Listen, o King. *To Radames.* You also, young hero, hear sage advice: they are enemies, and they are valiant ... they bear revenge in their hearts, emboldened by pardon, they will hasten to their arms again!

RADAMES: Spento Amonasro, il re guerrier, non resta speranza ai vinti.

With Amonasro, their warrior king, dead, no hope is left to the vanquished.

RAMPHIS: Almeno, arra di pace e sicurtà, fra noi resti col padre Aida.

At least, as a token of peace and security, let Aida's father remain among us.

KING: Al tuo consiglio io cedo. Di sicurtà, di pace un miglior pegno or io vo' darvi. Radames, la patria tutto a te deve. D'Amneris la mano premio ti sia. Sovra l'Egitto un giorno con essa regnerai.

I yield to your advice. Now I wish to give you a better pledge of security, of peace. Radames, your country owes you everything. Your reward shall be the hand of Amneris. One day you will reign over Egypt with her.

AMNERIS: Venga la schiava, venga a rapirmi l'amor mio ... se l'osa!

Aside. Let the slave come, let her come to seize my love from me ... if she dare!

KING & PEOPLE: Gloria all' Egitto, ad Iside che il sacro suol difende, s'intrecci il loto al lauro, s'intrecci il loto

Glory to Egypt, to Isis who protects its sacred soil, let lotus be interlaced with laurel, let lotus be interlaced with al lauro sul crin, sul crin del vincitor.

laurel on the brow, on the brow of the victor.

SLAVES & PRISONERS: Gloria al clemente Egizio che i nostri ceppi ha sciolto, che ci ridona ai liberi, che ci ridona ai liberi solchi del patrio suol.

Glory to the merciful Egyptian who has loosened our fetters, who returns us to the free, who returns us to the free furrows of our native soil.

RAMPHIS & PRIESTS: Inni levi-amo ad Iside che il sacro suol difende! Preghiam che i fati arridano, preghiam che i fati arridano fausti alla patria ognor.

Let us raise hymns to Isis who protects our sacrèd soil! Let us pray that the fates will assist, let us pray that the fates will always benevolently assist our country.

AIDA: Qual speme mai più restami? A lui . . . la gloria, il trono . . . a me l'oblio . . . le lacrime d'un disperato amor.

Aside. What hope is ever left for me? For him . . . glory, the throne . . . for me, oblivion . . . the tears of a hopeless love.

RADAMES: D'avverso Nume il folgore sul capo mio discende . . . ah no! d'Egitto il soglio non val . . . non val . . . non val . . . d'Aida il cor.

Aside. The thunderbolt of a hostile god descends on my head . . . ah no! Egypt's throne is not worth . . . is not worth . . . is not worth . . . as much as Aida's heart.

AMNERIS: Dall'inatteso giubilo inebbriata io sono; tutti in un dì si compiono i sogni del mio cor, i sogni del mio cor.

Aside. I am enraptured with unexpected joy; all my heart's dreams, my heart's dreams have been fulfilled in one day.

KING, PRIESTS & PEOPLE: Gloria ad Iside!

Glory to Isis!

RAMPHIS: Preghiam che i fati, preghiam che i fati arridano fausti alla patria ognor, fausti alla patria ognor.

Let us pray that the fates, let us pray that the benevolent fates will assist our country forever, our country forever.

KING & PEOPLE: Gloria! gloria!

Glory! glory!

AMONASRO: Fa cor: della tua patria i lieti eventi aspetta; per noi della vendetta già prossimo è l'albor.

To Aida. Take heart; expect good news from your country; the bright dawn of revenge is already close to us.

RADAMES: Qual inatteso folgore! qual inatteso folgore sul capo mio discende!

What an unexpected thunderbolt! what an unexpected thunderbolt descends on my head!

AMNERIS: Tutti in un dì si compiono le gioie del mio cor!

All my heart's joys are fulfilled in one day!

KING: Gloria all'Egitto! Gloria, gloria, gloria, gloria all'Egitto!

Glory to Egypt! Glory, glory, glory glory to Egypt!

AMONASRO: Fa cor, fa cor, fa cor, fa cor.

Take heart, take heart, take heart, take heart.

AIDA: A me l'oblio, a me l'oblio, le lacrime, le lacrime.

For me, oblivion, for me, oblivion, tears, tears.

RAMPHIS & BASS PRIESTS: Inni leviam ad Iside.

Let us raise hymns to Isis.

TENOR PRIESTS: Inni leviam, inni leviam.

Let us raise hymns, let us raise hymns.

PEOPLE: Gloria, gloria, gloria, gloria all'Egitto.

Glory, glory, glory, glory to Egypt.

AIDA: Ah! qual speme omai più restami? a lui . . . la gloria, il trono . . . a me . . . l'oblio, le lacrime d'un disperato amor, a me l'oblio, l'oblio, le lacrime d'un disperato amor, a me l'oblio,

Ah! what hope is ever left for me? for him . . . glory, the throne . . . for me, oblivion, the tears of a hopeless love, for me, oblivion, oblivion, the tears of a hopeless love, for me, oblivion, the tears of a

le lacrime d'un disperato amor.

hopeless love.

AMNERIS: Ah! dall'inatteso gaudio inebbriata io sono; tutte in un dì si compiono le gioie del mio cor, le gioie del mio cor, tutte del cor, tutte si compiono le gioie del mio cor, le gioie del mio cor, le gioie del cor.

I am enraptured with unexpected joy; in one day, all my heart's joys are fulfilled, my heart's joys, all my heart's, all my heart's joys are fulfilled, all my heart's joys, my heart's joys.

RADAMES: Ah! qual inatteso folgore sul capo mio discende! Ah no! d'Egitto il trono non val . . . non val . . . non val . . . d'Aida il cor, d'Egitto il suol non vale, non vale, non val d'Aida il cor, ah no, non val d'Aida il cor, d'Egitto il soglio non val d'Aida il cor, non val d'Aida il cor.

Ah! what an unexpected thunderbolt descends on my head! Ah no! Egypt's throne is not worth . . . not worth . . . not worth Aida's heart, Egypt's soil is not worth, not worth, not worth Aida's heart, ah no, it is not worth Aida's heart, Egypt's throne is not worth Aida's heart, not worth Aida's heart.

AMONASRO: Ah! fa cor, fa cor: la tua patria i lieti eventi aspetta; per noi della vendetta già prossimo è l'albor; per noi della, della vendetta già prossimo è l'albor, della vendetta già prossimo è l'albor, per noi, per noi della vendetta già prossimo è l'albor, per noi, per noi della vendetta già prossimo è l'albor, già prossimo è l'albor.

To Aida. Ah! take heart, take. heart: expect good news from your country; the bright dawn of revenge is already close to us, the bright dawn of revenge is already close to us, the bright dawn of revenge is already close to us, the bright dawn of revenge is already close to us, to us, to us, the bright dawn of revenge is already close, the bright dawn is already close.

KING & PEOPLE: Gloria, gloria all'Egitto, ad Iside che il

Glory, glory to Egypt, to Isis who protects its sacred soil!

sacro suol difende! S'intrecci il loto al lauro, s'intrecci il loto al lauro sul crin, sul crin del vincitor, s'intrecci il loto, il loto al lauro sul crin del vincitor, il loto al lauro sul crin del vincitor, s'intrecci il loto, il loto al lauro sul crin del vincitor, s'intrecci il loto, il loto al lauro sul crin del vincitor, sul crin del vincitor.

Let lotus be interlaced with laurel, let lotus be interlaced with laurel on the brow, on the brow of the victor, let lotus, lotus be interlaced with laurel on the brow of the victor, lotus with laurel on the brow of the victor, let lotus, lotus be interlaced with laurel on the brow of the victor, let lotus be interlaced, lotus with laurel, on the brow of the victor, on the brow of the victor.

RAMPHIS & PRIESTS: Inni leviamo ad Iside che il sacro suol difende! Preghiam che i fati arridano, preghiam che i fati arridano fausti alla patria, inni leviamo ad Iside, che il sacro suol, che il sacro suol difende, preghiam che i fati arridano fausti alla patria, alla patria ognor, preghiam, preghiam che i fati arridano fausti alla patria ognor, preghiam, preghiam che i fati arridano fausti alla patria ognor, fausti alla patria ognor.

Let us raise hymns to Isis who protects our sacred soil! Let us pray that the fates will assist, let us pray that the benevolent fates will assist our country, let us raise hymns to Isis who protects our sacred soil, our sacred soil, let us pray that the benevolent fates will assist our country, our country always, let us pray, let us pray that the benevolent fates will always assist our country, let us pray, let us pray that the benevolent fates will always assist our country, benevolent to our country always.

PRISONERS: Gloria al clemente Egizio che i nostri ceppi ha sciolto, che ci ridona ai liberi, che ci ridona ai liberi solchi del patrio suol, che ci ridona, ridona, che ci ridona ai

Glory to the merciful Egyptian who has loosened our fetters, who makes us free men again, who makes us free men again, tillers of our native soil, who makes us again, makes us, who makes us free men again,

liberi solchi del patrio suol, del patrio suol, gloria al clemente Egizio, gloria, gloria, gloria al clemente Egizio, gloria, gloria all' Egizio, gloria.

tillers of our native soil, our native soil, glory to the merciful Egyptian, glory, glory, glory to the Egyptian, glory.

SLAVES: Gloria al clemente Egizio che i nostri ceppi ha sciolto, che ci ridona ai liberi, che ci ridona ai liberi solchi del patrio suol, che ci ridona, ridona, che ci ridona ai liberi solchi del patrio suol, del patrio suol, del patrio suol, del patrio suol, del patrio, patrio suol.

Glory to the merciful Egyptian who has loosened our fetters, who makes us free men again, who makes us free men again, tillers of our native soil, who makes us again, makes us again, who makes us free men again, tillers of our native soil, our native soil, our native soil, our native soil, our native, native soil.

End of Act II

ACT THREE

ACT THREE

Some days later, late at night.

The banks of the Nile, near the Temple of Isis. After a brief orchestral introduction, voices can be heard chanting from inside the temple.

CHORUS: O tu che sei d'Osiride madre immortale e sposa, Diva che i casti palpiti desti agli umani in cor . . .

O thou who art immortal mother and wife of Osiris, goddess who awakest the chaste throbbing of human hearts. . . .

GRAND PRIESTESS: Soccorri, soccorri a noi . . .

Give succour, give succour to us. . . .

CHORUS: Soccorri a noi pietosa, madre d'immenso amor . . .

Give succour to us in your pity, great loving mother. . . .

PRIESTESS & CHORUS: —soccorri a noi, soccorri a noi . . .

—give succour to us, give succour to us. . . .

A boat glides down the river. Ramphis and Amneris alight, attended by guards and heavily veiled women.

RAMPHIS: Vieni d'Iside al tempio: alla vigilia delle tue nozze invoca della Diva il favore. Iside legge de' mortali nel core: ogni mistero degli umani a lei [è] noto.

Come to the temple of Isis: invoke the goddess's favor on the eve of your nuptials. Isis reads into mortal hearts: every human secret is known to her.

AMNERIS: Sì; io pregherò che Radames mi doni tutto il suo cor . . . come il mio cor a lui sacro è per sempre . . .

Yes; I shall pray that Radames may give me his whole heart . . . as my heart is forever sacred to him. . . .

RAMPHIS: Andiamo. Pregherai fino all'alba; io sarò teco.

Let us go. You will pray until dawn; I shall be with you.

Ramphis, Amneris, and attendants enter the temple.

PRIESTESSES: Soccorri, soccorri a noi . . .

Give succour, give succour to us. . . .

CHORUS: Soccorri a noi pietosa, madre d'immenso amor—

Give succour to us pitiable ones, great loving mother—

PRIESTESSES & CHORUS: Soccorri a noi, soccorri a noi.

Give succour to us, give succour to us.

Aida, veiled, appears surreptitiously.

AIDA: Qui Radames verrà! Che vorrà dirmi? Io tremo! Ah! se tu vieni a recarmi, o crudel, l'ultimo addio, del Nilo i cupi vortici mi daran tomba . . . e pace forse . . . e pace forse e oblio.

Oh patria mia, mai più, mai più ti rivedrò! mai più! mai più ti rivedrò! O cieli azzurri, o dolci aure native, dove sereno il mio mattin brillò . . . o verdi colli, o profumate rive, o patria mia, mai più ti rivedrò! Oh patria mia, mai più, ah! mai più, mai più ti rivedrò! Oh patria mia, oh patria mia, mai più ti rivedrò, mai più! no . . . no . . . mai più, mai più! O fresche valli, o queto asil beato che un dì promesso dall'amor mi fu . . . Or che d'amore

Radames is coming here! What will he tell me? I tremble! Ah! if you come, oh cruel one, to bid me the last farewell, the Nile's deep whirlpools will be my grave . . . and perhaps peace . . . and perhaps peace and oblivion.

Oh, my country, I shall never more, never more see you again! never more! I shall never more see you again! Oh blue skies, oh sweet native breezes, where my dawn sparkled gently. . . . Oh green hills, oh fragrant shores, oh my country, I shall never more see you again! Oh my country, never more, ah! I shall never more, never more see you again! Oh my country, oh my country, I shall never more see you again, never more! no . . . no . . . never more, never more. Oh

Act 3. The "Nile Scene." Margherita Roberti as Aida sings "O Patria Mia," in which she describes the beautiful homeland she fears she will never see again.

(Museum of the Bolshoi Theater, Moscow)

Act 3. The "Nile Scene." Ramphis and Amneris enter the temple.

il sogno è dileguato . . . o
patria mia, non ti vedrò
mai più! oh patria mia, non
ti vedrò mai più! no . . .
mai più . . . non ti vedrò,
non ti vedrò mai più! oh
patria mia, mai più . . . ti
rivedrò!

fresh vales, oh blessed quiet
refuge that my love once
promised me . . . now that
love's dream is faded . . . oh
my country, I shall never
more see you! oh my country,
I shall never more see you!
no . . . never more . . . I shall
never more see you, I shall
never more see you! oh my
country, I shall never more
see you!

Amonasro enters furtively.

AIDA: Ciel! mio padre!

Heavens! my father!

AMONASRO: A te grave cagion
m'adduce, Aida. Nulla
sfugge al mio sguardo.
D'amor ti struggi per
Radames . . . ei t'ama . . .
qui lo attendi. Dei Faraon la
figlia è tua rivale . . . razza
infame, aborrita, e a noi
fatale!

A solemn reason brings me to
you, Aida. Nothing escapes
my notice. You are consumed
with love for Radames . . . he
loves you . . . you await him
here. The Pharaoh's daughter
is your rival . . . infamous,
hated race, deadly to us!

AIDA: E in suo potere io sto!
Io d'Amonasro figlia!

And I am in her power! I, the
daughter of Amonasro!

AMONASRO: In poter di lei!
No . . . se lo brami, la possente rival tu vincerai, e
patria, e trono, e amor,
tutto tu avrai. Rivedrai le
foreste imbalsamate, le
fresche valli, i nostri templi
d'or!

In the power of that one! No
. . . if you wish, you shall con-
quer your mighty rival, and
you shall have your country,
your throne, and love, all
these things. You shall see the
fragrant forests again, the
fresh vales, our golden
temples!

AIDA: Rivedrò le foreste imbalsamate! le fresche valli
. . . i nostri templi d'or!

Happily. I shall see the fragrant
forests again! the fresh vales
. . . our golden temples!

AMONASRO: Sposa felice a lui che amasti tanto, tripudii immensi ivi potrai gioir . . .

Happy wife to him whom you have loved so much, there you can enjoy great triumph. . . .

AIDA: Un giorno solo di sì dolce incanto . . . un'ora, un'ora di tal gioia e poi morir! e poi morir!

Only one day of such sweet enchantment . . . one hour, one hour of such joy, and then to die! and then to die!

AMONASRO: Pur rammenti che a noi l'Egizio immite le case, i tempii e l'are profanò . . . trasse in ceppi le vergini rapite . . . madri . . . vecchi . . . fanciulli ei trucidò.

Yet remember that the merciless Egyptian has desecrated our houses, our temples, our altars . . . carried our maidens off in chains . . . has slain mothers . . . the aged . . . the young.

AIDA: Ah! ben rammento quegl'infausti giorni! rammento i lutti che il mio cor soffrì! Deh! fate o Numi, che per noi ritorni,—

Ah! I well remember those unhappy days! I remember the sorrows that my heart suffered! Ah! . . . fates or gods, let a dawn,—

AMONASRO: Rammenta!

Remember!

AIDA: —che per noi ritorni l'alba invocata de'sereni dì.

—that heralds peaceful days return for us, let it return for us.

AMONASRO: Non fia che tardi. In armi ora si desta il popol nostro; tutto è pronto già . . . Vittoria avrem . . . Solo a saper mi resta qual sentier il nemico seguirà . . .

It will not delay. Our people are now provoked to arms; everything will soon be ready . . . . We shall be victorious . . . . The only thing left for me to know is which path the enemy will follow. . . .

AIDA: Chi scoprir lo potria? chi mai?

Who can find it out? Whoever?

AMONASRO: Tu stessa!

You yourself!

AIDA: Io!

I!

AMONASRO: Radames so che qui attendi . . . Ei t'ama . . . ei conduce gli Egizii . . . Intendi?

I know that you await Radames here . . . he loves you . . . he leads the Egyptians. . . . Do you understand?

AIDA: Orrore! Che mi consigli tu? No! no! giammai!

Horror! What are you suggesting to me? No! no! never!

AMONASRO: Su, dunque! sorgete, egizie coorti! col fuoco struggete le nostre città . . . Spargete il terrore, le stragi, le morti, al vostro furore più freno non v'ha.

Come, then! arise, Egyptian cohorts! destroy our cities with fire. . . . Spread terror, destruction, death. . . there is nothing to stop your fury.

AIDA: Ah! padre! padre!

Ah! father! father!

Amonasro rejects Aida.

AMONASRO: Mia figlia ti chiami!

You call yourself—my daughter!

AIDA: Pietà! pietà! pietà!

Pity! pity! pity!

AMONASRO: Flutti di sangue scorrono sulle città dei vinti . . . Vedi? dai negri vortici si levano gli estinti . . . ti additan essi e gridano: *per te la patria muor!*

Rivers of blood run over the cities of the vanquished. . . . You see? The dead rise out of their dark depths . . . pointing at you and crying: *because of you, our country is slain!*

AIDA: Pietà! pietà! padre, pietà!

Pity! pity! father, pity!

AMONASRO: Una larva orribile fra l'ombre a noi s'affaccia . . . trema! le scarne braccia . . .

A horrible phantom reveals itself to us among the shadows . . . tremble! its emaciated arms. . . .

AIDA: Ah!

Ah!

AMONASRO: —sul capo tuo levò . . .

—it lifts over your head. . . .

AIDA: Padre!

Father!

AMONASRO: Tua madre ell'è—

It is your mother—

AIDA: No!

No!

AMONASRO: —ravvisala—

—look at her—

AIDA: Ah!

Ah!

AMONASRO: —ti maledice . . .

—she curses you—

AIDA: Ah! no! ah! no! padre, pietà! pietà! pietà! pietà! pietà!

Ah! no! Ah! no! father, pity! pity! pity! pity! pity!

Amonasro again rejects the terrified Aida's entreaties.

AMONASRO: Non sei mia figlia . . . Dei Faraoni tu sei la schiava!

You are not my daughter. . . . You are the slave of the Pharaohs!

AIDA: Ah! pietà! pietà! pietà! Padre! a costoro schiava non sono . . . Non maledirmi . . . non imprecarmi . . . ancor tua figlia potrai chiamarmi . . . della mia patria, della mia patria degna sarò.

Ah! pity! pity! pity! Father! I am not the slave of tha folk . . . do not curse me . . . do not condemn me . . . you shall still be able to call me your daughter . . . I shall be worthy of my country, of my country.

AMONASRO: Pensa che un popolo vinto, straziato per te soltanto, per te soltanto risorger può . . .

Remember that a defeated people, mangled because of you alone, because of you alone, can rise again. . . .

AIDA: Oh patria! oh patria! . . . quanto mi costi! oh patria! quanto mi costi!

Oh my country! oh my country . . . how much you ask of me! oh my country! how much you ask of me!

AMONASRO: Coraggio! ei giunge . . . là tutto udrò.

Courage! he approaches . . . I shall hear everything over there.

Amonasro hides among the palms as Radames enters.

RADAMES: Pur ti riveggo, mia dolce Aida.

But to see you again, my sweet Aida.

AIDA: T'arresta, vanne . . .
che speri ancor?

Stop, go away . . . what do you
yet hope for?

RADAMES: A te dappresso
l'amor mi guida.

Love leads me to your side.

AIDA: Te i riti attendono d'un
altro amor. D'Amneris
sposo . . .

The rites of another love await
you. Husband of Amneris. . . .

RADAMES: Che parli mai? Te
sola, Aida, te deggio amar
. . . Gli Dei m'ascoltano
. . . tu mia sarai.

Whatever are you saying? I
must love only you, Aida . . .
the gods are listening to me
. . . you shall be mine.

AIDA: D'uno spergiuro non
ti macchiar! Prode t'amai,
non t'amerei spergiuro.

Do not besmirch yourself with
perjury! I loved you as a hero,
I would not love you forsworn.

RADAMES: Dell'amor mio
dubiti, Aida?

Do you question my love,
Aida?

AIDA: E come speri sottrarti
d'Amneris ai vezzi, del Re
al voler, del tuo popolo ai
voti, dei Sacerdoti all'ira?

And how do you hope to
escape the cajoleries of Amneris, the command of the
King, the vows of your people,
the wrath of the priests?

RADAMES: Odimi, Aida. Nel
fiero anelito di nuova guerra
il suolo Etiope si ridestò . . .
I tuoi già invadono la
nostra terra, io degli Egizi
duce sarò. Fra il suon, fra i
plausi della vittoria, al Re
mi prostro, gli svelo il cor
. . . Sarai tu il serto della
mia gloria, vivrem beati
d'eterno amore. Sarai tu
il serto della mia gloria,
vivrem beati d'eterno amor.

Listen to me, Aida. The
Ethiopian land has again
roused itself to the fierce
anticipation of a fresh war. . . .
Your people have already
invaded our land, I shall be
leader of the Egyptians.
Among the noise, among the
praises of victory, I shall pros-
trate myself before the King,
I shall bare my heart to
him . . . you will be the garland of my glory, we shall live
happily in eternal love. You

will be the garland of my glory, we shall live happily in eternal love.

AIDA: Nè d'Amneris paventi il vindice furor? La sua vendetta, come folgor tremenda cadrà su me, sul padre mio, su tutti.

And do you not fear Amneris's vindictive fury? Like a terrible thunderbolt, her revenge will fall on me, on my father, on everyone.

RADAMES: Io vi difendo.

I shall protect you.

AIDA: Invan! Tu nol potresti . . . Pur se tu m'ami ancor s'apre una via di scampo a noi . . .

In vain! You could not . . . but if you still love me, one way of escape is open to us. . . .

RADAMES: Quale?

What?

AIDA: Fuggir.

To flee.

RADAMES: Fuggire!

To flee!

AIDA: Fuggiam gli ardori inospiti di queste lande ignude; una novella patria al nostro amor si schiude . . . Là tra foreste vergini, di fiori profumate, in estasi beate la terra scorderem, in estasi, in estasi la terra scorderem.

Let us flee the unkind heat of these barren deserts; a new country is open to our love. . . . There, among virgin forests, among perfumed flowers, in our blessed rapture we shall forget the world, in rapture, in rapture we shall forget the world.

RADAMES: Sovra una terra estranea teco fuggir dovrei! abbandonar la patria, l'are de'nostri Dei! il suol dov'io raccolsi di gloria i primi allori, il ciel de'nostri amori come scordar potrem?

I should flee with you to a strange land! abandon my country, the altars of our gods! how could we forget the soil where I reaped the first wreaths of glory, the heaven of our love?

AIDA: Là tra foreste vergini, di fiori profumate, in estasi

There, among the virgin forests, among perfumed

beate la terra scorderem, in estasi, in estasi la terra scorderem. Sotto il mio ciel, più libero l'amor ne fia concesso; ivi nel tempio istesso gli stessi Numi avrem, ivi nel tempio istesso gli stessi Numi avrem, ivi nel tempio istesso gli stessi Numi avrem, fuggiam, fuggiam . . .

flowers, we shall forget the world in blessed rapture, in ecstasy. Under my skies we could enjoy a freer love; there, in the same temple, we shall have the same gods, thére in the same temple, we shall have the same gods, there, in the same temple, we shall have the same gods, let us flee, let us flee.

RADAMES: Il ciel de'nostri amori come scordar potrem? Come scordar? come scordar potrem il ciel de'nostri amor? il ciel de'nostri amori come scordar potrem? Abbandonar la patria, l'are de'nostri Dei! il ciel de'nostri amori come scordar potrem? Aida!

How could we forget the heaven of our love? How could we forget? How could we forget the heaven of our love? How could we forget the heaven of our love? To abandon my country, the altars of our gods! how could we forget the heaven of our love? Aida!

AIDA: Tu non m'ami . . .Va!

You do not love me. . . . Go!

RADAMES: Non t'amo!

I do not love you!

AIDA: Va!

Go!

RADAMES: Mortal giammai nè Dio arse d'amor al par del mio possente.

Neither god nor mortal ever burned with such powerful love as mine.

AIDA: Va . . . va . . . t'attende all'ara Amneris.

Go . . . go . . . Amneris awaits you at the altar.

RADAMES: No! giammai!

No! never!

AIDA: Giammai, dicesti? Allor . . . piombi la scure su me, sul padre mio . . .

Never, did you say? Then . . . may the axe descend on me, on my father. . . .

RADAMES: Ah no! fuggiamo! Sì: fuggiam da queste mura, al deserto insiem fuggiamo; qui sol regna la sventura, là si schiude un ciel d'amor. I deserti interminati a noi talamo saranno, su noi gli astri brilleranno di più limpido fulgor.

Ah no! let us flee. Yes: let us flee from these walls, let us flee together to the desert; here, only misfortune reigns, there a heaven of love will open up. The endless deserts will be our nuptial bed . . . the stars will shine on us with a clearer fire.

AIDA: Nella terra avventurata de'miei padri, il ciel ne attende; ivi l'aura è imbalsamata, ivi il suolo è aromi e fior. Fresche valli e verdi prati a noi talamo saranno, su noi gli astri brilleranno di più limpido fulgor.

Heaven awaits us in my ancestors' blessed land; the breeze is fragrant there, the earth is perfumed with flowers there. Fresh vales and green meadows will be our nuptial bed, and the stars will shine on us with clearer fire.

AIDA & RADAMES: Vieni meco, insiem fuggiamo questa terra di dolor . . . Vieni meco, t'amo, t'amo! a noi duce fia l'amor, fia l'amor.

Come with me, together let us flee this land of sorrow . . . come with me, I love you, I love you! let love be our guide, let love be our guide.

AIDA: Ma, dimmi: per qual via eviterem le schiere degli armati?

But, tell me: on which road shall we avoid the legions of armed men?

RADAMES: Il sentier scelto dai nostri a piombar sul nemico fia deserto fino a domani . . .

The path our men have chosen to descend upon the enemy will be deserted until tomorrow. . . .

AIDA: E quel sentier?

And that path?

RADAMES: Le gole di Napatà . .

The gorges of Napata. . . .

Amonasro steps from concealment.

AMONASRO: Di Napatà le gole! ivi saranni i miei . . .

The gorges of Napata! My men will be there. . . .

RADAMES: Oh! chi ci ascolta?

Oh! who heard us?

AMONASRO: D'Aida il padre, e degli Etiopi il Re.

The father of Aida and the King of the Ethiopians.

RADAMES: Tu! Amonasro? tu! il Re? Numi! che dissi? No . . . non è ver . . . non è ver . . . non è ver . . . no . . . no . . . no . . . non è ver . . . no! sogno,delirio è questo . .

You! Amonasro! you! the King? gods! what did I say? No . . . it is not true . . . it is not true . . . it is not true . . . no, no, no, it is not true . . . no! this is a mad dream. . . .

AIDA: Ah no! ti calma, ascoltami . . .

Ah no! calm yourself, listen to me. . . .

AMONASRO: A   te   l'amor d'Aida—

Aida's love for you—

AIDA: —all'amor mio t'affida.

—have faith in my love.

AMONASRO: —un   soglio innalzerà.

—will raise you to a throne.

RADAMES: Io son disonorato! Io son disonorato! Per te tradii la patria! Tradii la patria!

I am dishonored! I am dishonored! I betrayed my country for you! I betrayed my country!

AIDA: Ti calma!

Calm yourself!

AMONASRO: No: tu non sei colpevole, non sei colpevole: era voler, era voler del fato . . .

No: you are not guilty, you arc not guilty: it was the will, it was the will of fate. . . .

RADAMES: Io son disonorato! Io son disonorato! Per te tradii la patria! Per te tradii la patria!

I am dishonored! I am dishonored! I betrayed my country for you! I betrayed my country for you!

AIDA: Ah no! ah no! ti calma!

Ah no! ah no! calm yourself!

AMONASRO: No! No! No! Tu non sei colpevole. Vien: oltre il Nil ne attendono i prodi a noi devoti,

No! No! No! You are not, you are not guilty. Come: the gallant men devoted to us are waiting for us

là del tuo cor, del tuo
cuore i voti coronerà l'amor.
Vieni, vieni, vieni.

there beyond the Nile, there
love will crown the vows of
your heart, of your heart.
Come, come, come.

He tries to force Radames to accompany him, as Amneris calls from the temple.

AMNERIS: Traditor!

Traitor!

AIDA: La mia rival!

My rival!

AMONASRO: L'opra mia a
strugger vieni! Muori!

You come to destroy my plan!
Die!

Dagger in hand, he starts toward Amneris. Radames rushes between them.

RADAMES: Arresta, insano!

Stop, madman!

AMNERIS: Oh rabbia!

Oh fury!

Ramphis appears from the temple.

RAMPHIS: Guardie, olà!

Guards, hey there!

RADAMES: Presto! Fuggite!

To Aida and Amonasro. Quickly!
Fly!

AMONASRO: Vieni, o figlia.

Come, o daughter.

He tries to pull Aida with him.

RAMPHIS: L'inseguite!

To guards. Follow them!

RADAMES: Sacerdote, io resto
a te.

To Ramphis. Priest, I remain at
your mercy.

End of Act III

ACT FOUR
Scene One

(Verdi nelle Immagini)

Villa and gardens at Verdi's Sant'Agata retreat, today a national shrine.

(Verdi nelle Immagini)

ACT FOUR
Scene One

A short time later, in a hall in the palace of the King of Egypt.

On one side is a large doorway, leading to the underground court and trial rooms; on the other side, a corridor leading to the cell where RADAMES is imprisoned. AMNERIS mournfully stands in front of the doorway as the curtain rises.

AMNERIS: L'aborrita rivale a me sfuggia . . . Dai sacerdoti Radames attende dei traditor la pena. Traditor egli non è . . . Pur rivelò di guerra l'alto segreto . . . egli fuggir volea . . . con lei fuggire . . . Traditori tutti! A morte! A morte! Oh! che mai parlo? Io l'amo, io l'amo sempre . . . Disperato, insano è quest'amor che la mia vita strugge. Oh! s'ei potesse amarmi! Vorrei salvarlo! E come? Si tenti! Guardie: Radames qui venga.

My hated rival has fled. . . . Radames awaits a traitor's penalty from the priests. He is not a traitor . . . yet he did reveal a high secret of war . . . he wanted to flee . . . to flee with her. . . . Traitors all! Death to them! Death to them! Oh! What am I saying? I love him, I shall always love him . . . Mad, hopeless is this love that is destroying my life. Oh! if he could love me! I would save him! And how? I shall attempt it! Guards: let Radames come here.

The guards exit and re-enter, followed by Radames.

Già i sacerdoti adunansi arbitri del tuo fato; pur dell'accusa orribile scolparti ancor t'è dato; ti scolpa e la tua grazia io pregherò dal trono, e nun-

The priests have already gathered to judge your fate; but you still have a chance to clear yourself of the awful accusation; clear yourself and I shall pray the throne's favor

127

zia di perdono, e nunzia di perdono, di vita a te sarò.

for you, and I shall be your ambassador for pardon, your ambassador for pardon and for life.

RADAMES: Di mie discolpe i giudici mai non udran l'accento; dinanzi ai Numi, agl'uomini nè vil, nè reo mi sento. Profferse il labbro incauto fatal segreto, è vero, ma puro il mio pensiero, ma puro il mio pensiero, e l'onor mio restò.

The judges will not hear a word of excuse from me; I consider myself neither base nor guilty before gods and men. My careless lips gave up the fatal secret, it is true, but my intent was pure, my intent pure, and my honor remained.

AMNERIS: Salvati dunque e scolpati.

Then attest your innocence and save yourself.

RADAMES: No.

No.

AMNERIS: Tu morrai.

You will die.

RADAMES: La vita aborro; d'ogni gaudio la fonte inaridita, svanita ogni speranza, sol bramo di morir.

I hate life; the fountain of every joy has dried up, every hope has vanished, I desire only to die.

AMNERIS: Morire! Ah! . . . tu dei vivere! Sì, all'amor mio vivrai; per te le angoscie orribili di morte io già provai; t'amai, soffersi tanto . . . vegliai le notti in pianto . . . e patria, e trono, e trono e vita, tutto darei, tutto, tutto darei per te.

To die! Ah! . . . you must live! Yes, you shall live for my love; I have already suffered the dreadful pangs of death for you; I loved you . . . I have suffered so much . . . I spent the nights awake, weeping . . . and I would give up my country, the throne, the throne, my life, everything, everything, I would give up everything for you.

RADAMES: Per essa anch'io la patria, per essa anch'io la

I even betrayed my country for her, even for her my country,

A caricature of Verdi by Enrico Caruso. From *Caricatures by Enrico Caruso*, published by "La Follia di New York," 1922. Courtesy of the publisher.

patria e l'onor mio, e l'onor mio tradia . . .

AMNERIS: Di lei non più!

RADAMES: L'infamia m'attende e vuoi ch'io viva? Misero appien mi festi, Aida a me togliesti, spenta l'hai forse . . . e in dono offri la vita a me?

AMNERIS: Io . . . di sua morte origine! No! Vive Aida . . .

RADAMES: Vive!

AMNERIS: Nei disperati aneliti dell'orde fuggitive sol cadde il padre . . .

RADAMES: Ed ella?

AMNERIS: Sparve, nè più novella s'ebbe . . .

RADAMES: Gli Dei l'adducano salva alle patrie mura, e ignori la sventura di chi per lei morrà!

AMNERIS: Ma, s'io ti salvo, giurami che più non la vedrai . . .

RADAMES: Nol posso!

AMNERIS: A lei rinunzia per sempre . . . e tu vivrai!

RADAMES: Nol posso!

AMNERIS: Anco una volta: a lei rinunzia . . .

and my honor for her, and my honor for her. . . .

No more of her!

Disgrace awaits me and you want me to live? You made me completely miserable, you took Aida from me, perhaps you have killed her . . . and as a gift you offer me life?

I . . . the cause of her death! No! Aida lives. . . .

She lives!

Only her father was killed in the desperate panting flight of the fleeing hordes. . . .

And she?

She disappeared, nor has there been any more news of her. . . .

May the gods lead her safely to her country's borders, and may she never know the ill luck of him who will die for her!

But if I save you, swear to me that you will never see her again. . . .

I cannot!

Renounce her forever, and you shall live!

I cannot!

Once again: renounce her. . . .

RADAMES: È vano . . .

It is in vain. . . .

AMNERIS: Morir vuoi dunque, insano?

Then you would die, madman?

RADAMES: Pronto a morir son già.

I am already prepared to die.

AMNERIS: Chi ti salva, sciagurato, dalla sorte che t'aspetta? In furore hai tu cangiato un amor ch'egual non ha. De'miei pianti la vendetta or dal ciel si compirà, de'miei pianti la vendetta or dal ciel . . . dal ciel si compirà.

Who will save you, wretched man, from the fate that awaits you? Into rage you have altered a love that has no match. My tears will now be avenged by heaven, my tears now avenged by heaven . . . will now be avenged by heaven, now by heaven.

RADAMES: È la morte un ben supremo se per lei—

Death is a supreme blessing if—

AMNERIS: Ah! chi ti salva?

Ah! who will save you?

RADAMES: —morir m'è dato; nel subir l'estremo fato gaudii immensi il cor avrà—

—I am able to die for her; my heart will have great joy in bearing its final fate—

AMNERIS: De'miei pianti la vendetta or dal ciel . . . ciel . . . dal ciel si compirà. De' miei pianti la vendetta or dal ciel si compirà.

My tears will now be avenged by heaven . . . heaven . . . will be avenged by heaven. My tears will now be avenged by heaven.

RADAMES: —gaudii immensi il cor avrà. L'ira umana più non temo, temo sol la tua pietà; l'ira umana più non temo, temo sol la tua pietà.

—my heart will have great joy. I no longer fear human wrath, I only fear your mercy; I no longer fear human wrath, I only fear your mercy.

Exit Radames, attended by guards. Amneris collapses into a chair.

AMNERIS: Ohimè! morir mi sento . . . Oh! chi lo salva? E in poter di costoro io

Oh woe! I feel myself dying. . . Oh! who will save him? And I myself have cast him into their

stessa lo gettai! Ora, a te impreco atroce gelosia, che la sua morte e il lutto eterno del mio cor segnasti!

power of those men! Now I curse you, awful jealousy, who have marked him for death and my heart for eternal mourning!

The priests cross the stage to the judgment chambers; Amneris sees them.

AMNERIS: Ecco i fatali, gl' inesorati ministri di morte . . . Oh! ch'io non vegga quelle bianche larve!

Here are the fatal, the inexorable ministers of death. . . . Oh! that I might not see those white phantoms!

She hides her face in her hands.

E in poter di costoro io stessa lo gettai! io stessa! io stessa lo gettai! e in poter di costoro io stessa lo gettai!

And I myself cast him into their power! I myself! I myself cast him! and I myself cast him into their power!

The voices of Ramphis and the priests are heard from offstage.

RAMPHIS & PRIESTS: Spirto del Nume sovra noi discendi! ne avviva al raggio dell' eterna luce; pel labbro nostro tua giustizia apprendi . . .

May the spirit of the god descend upon us! vivify us in the ray of eternal light; learn your punishment through our lips. . . .

AMNERIS: Numi, pietà del mio straziato core . . . Egli è innocente, lo salvate, o Numi! Disperato, tremendo è il mio dolore!

Gods, pity my tortured heart. . . . He is innocent, save him, o gods! Desperate, boundless is my sorrow.

Radames re-enters, accompanied by guards, and is conducted to the judgment chambers.

RAMPHIS & PRIESTS: Spirto del Nume—

May the spirit of the god—

AMNERIS: Oh! chi lo salva?

Sees Radames. Oh! who will save him?

RAMPHIS & PRIESTS: —sovra noi discendi!

—descend upon us!

AMNERIS: Oh! chi lo salva? Mi sento morir! Ohimè! Ohimè! Mi sento morir!

Oh! who will save him? I am dying! Oh woe! Oh woe! I am dying!

Ramphis and the priests are again heard from offstage.

RAMPHIS: Radames! Radames! Radames! Tu rivelasti della patria i segreti allo straniero . . . Discolpati.

Radames! Radames! Radames! You revealed your country's secrets to the foreigner . . . Clear yourself.

PRIESTS: Discolpati!

Clear yourself!

RAMPHIS: Egli tace. . . .

He is silent. . . .

RAMPHIS & PRIESTS: Traditor!

Traitor!

AMNERIS: Ah pietà! Egli è innocente, Numi, pietà, Numi, pietà!

Ah pity! He is innocent, gods, pity, gods, pity!

RAMPHIS: Radames! Radames! Radames! Tu disertasti dal campo il dì che precedea la pugna . . . Discolpati!

Radames! Radames! Radames! You deserted the field on the day before battle . . . Clear yourself!

PRIESTS: Discolpati!

Clear yourself!

RAMPHIS: Egli tace. . . .

He is silent. . . .

PRIESTS: Traditor!

Traitor!

AMNERIS: Ah pietà! Ah! lo salvate, Numi, pietà, Numi, pietà!

Ah pity! ah! save him, gods, pity, gods, pity!

RAMPHIS: Radames! Radames Radames! Tua fè violasti, alla patria spergiuro, al Re, all'onor . . . Discolpati!

Radames! Radames! Radames! You violated your trust, forswore your country, your king, honor . . . Clear yourself!

PRIESTS: Discolpati!

Clear yourself!

RAMPHIS: Egli tace. . . .

He is silent. . . .

RAMPHIS & PRIESTS: Traditor!

Traitor!

AMNERIS: Ah pietà! Ah! Lo salvate, Numi, pietà, Numi, pietà!

Ah pity! Ah! Save him, gods, pity, gods, pity!

RAMPHIS & PRIESTS: Radames ... è deciso il tuo fato; degli infami la morte tu avrai; sotto l'ara del Nume sdegnato, sotto l'ara del Nume sdegnato a te vivo fia schiuso l'avel. ...

Radames . . . your fate is settled; you will have the death of disgraced men; under the altar of the god you have scorned, under the altar of the god you have scorned, a living grave will be opened for you. . . .

AMNERIS: A lui vivo la tomba . . . oh! gl'infami! nè di sangue son paghi giammai . . . e si chiaman ministri del ciel!

A living grave for him . . . oh! those infamous men! nor are they ever sated with blood . . . and they call themselves ministers of heaven!

The priests begin to file back out.

RAMPHIS & PRIESTS: Traditor! Traditor! Traditor!

Traitor! Traitor! Traitor!

Amneris flings herself in their path.

AMNERIS: Sacerdoti: compiste un delitto! Tigri infami di sangue assetate . . . voi la terra ed i Numi oltraggiate . . . punite chi colpe non ha.

Priests: you have committed a crime! Infamous tigers, thirsting for blood . . . you outrage earth and the gods . . . you punish one who is guiltless.

RAMPHIS: È traditor!

He is a traitor!

PRIESTS: È traditor!

He is a traitor!

RAMPHIS & PRIESTS: Morrà.

He must die.

AMNERIS: Sacerdote: quest' uomo che uccidi, tu lo sai . . . da me un giorno fu amato . . . L'anatema d'un core straziato col suo sangue su te ricadrà!

To Ramphis. Priest: this man whom you kill, you know . . . once he was beloved by me . . . the curse of a broken heart will fall on you with his blood!

RAMPHIS: È traditor!

He is a traitor!

PRIESTS: È traditor!

He is a traitor!

RAMPHIS & PRIESTS: Morrà!

He must die!

AMNERIS: Voi la terra ed i Numi oltraggiate . . . voi punite, punite chi colpe non ha.

You outrage earth and gods . . . you punish, you punish one who is guiltless.

RAMPHIS & PRIESTS: È traditor! Morrà! Morrà! È traditor! È traditor! Morrà! È traditor! Morrà, morrà! È traditor! Morrà, morrà! È traditor! Morrà! Morrà!

He is a traitor! He must die! He must die! He is a traitor! He is a traitor! He must die! He is a traitor! He must die, he must die! He is a traitor! He must die, he must die! He is a traitor! he must die! He must die!

AMNERIS: Ah no, ah no, non è, non è, ah no, non è, no no non è traditor, ah no, ah no, non è traditor! Ah no, ah no, non è traditor . . . pietà, pietà, pietà, pietà!

Ah no, ah no, he is not, he is not, ah no, he is not, no, no, he is not a traitor, ah no, ah no, he is not a traitor! Ah no, ah no, he is not a traitor! ah no, ah no, he is not a traitor . . . pity! pity! pity! pity!

Ramphis and the priests finish crossing the stage and exit.

RAMPHIS & PRIESTS: Traditor! Traditor! Traditor!

Traitor! Traitor! Traitor!

AMNERIS: Empia razza! Anatema su voi! la vendetta del ciel, del ciel . . . scenderà! Anatema su voi!

Impious breed! A curse on you! The heavens', the heavens' revenge will descend! A curse on you!

ACT FOUR
Scene Two

(Lyric Opera of Chicago. Photo by Nancy Sorensen)

Act 4, Scene 2. In the "Entombment Scene," Aida and Radames, sealed in a vault, sing their farewell to earth while Amneris, kneeling on the stone that seals the vault, pleads for herself and for Radames. In this 1960 production, Margherita Roberti and Carlo Bergonzi portray Aida and Radames and Giulietta Simionato is Amneris.

ACT FOUR

Scene Two

A short time later, in the Temple of Vulcan.

The stage is divided into two horizontal levels. The upper level is the interior of the temple, glittering and ornate. The lower level is a gloomy vault, supported by pillars, which, in turn, are supported by statues. RADAMES is on the stairs leading down into the vault. Over him, two priests are just finishing moving into place the stone which seals the vault.

RADAMES: La fatal pietra sovra me si chiuse . . . Ecco la tomba mia. Del dì la luce più non vedrò . . . non rivedrò più Aida . . . Aida, ove sei tu? Possa tu almeno viver felice e la mia sorte orrenda sempre ignorar!

The fatal stone has closed over me. . . . This is my tomb. I shall never again see the light of day. . . . I shall never more see Aida. . . . Aida, where are you? May you at least live happily and ever in ignorance of my awful fate!

He sees a shadowy form moving in the vault.

Qual gemito! Una larva . . . una vision . . . No! forma umana è questa . . . Ciel! Aida!

What moan! A phantom . . . a vision. . . .
No! it is a human shape. . . .
Heavens! Aida!

Aida emerges from where she has been hiding in the gloom. Radames approaches her with a combination of joy and despair.

AIDA: Son io.

It is I.

RADAMES: Tu . . . in questa tomba!

You . . . in this tomb!

AIDA: Presago il core della tua condanna, in questa tomba che per te s'apriva io penetrai furtiva ... e qui lontana da ogni umano sguardo nelle tue braccia desiai morire.

Unhappily. My heart forboded your sentence, I furtively entered this tomb which was opened for you ... and here, far from human sight, I wanted to die in your arms.

RADAMES: Morir! sì pura e bella! morir . . . per me d'amore ... degli anni tuoi nel fiore, degl'anni tuoi nel fiore fuggir la vita! T'avea il cielo per l'amor creata, ed io t'uccido per averti amata! No, non morrai! troppo t'amai! troppo sei bella!

To die! so pure and lovely! to die ... for love of me ... to flee from life in the flower of your years, in the flower of your years! Heaven created you for love, and I murder you by having loved you! No, you shall not die! I have loved you too much! You are too beautiful!

AIDA: Vedi? Di morte l'angelo radiante a noi s'appressa ... ne adduce a eterni gaudii sovra i suoi vanni d'or ... Già veggo il ciel dischiudersi ... ivi ogni affanno cessa ... ivi comincia l'estasi d'un immortale amor.... comincia l'estasi d'un immortale amor.

Do you see? The radiant angel of death is coming toward us ... it will carry us from here to eternal bliss on its huge golden wings. ... Already I see heaven opening up ... every sorrow will cease there ... the rapture of an immortal love will begin there ... the rapture of an immortal love will begin.

On the upper level, priests and priestesses begin to chant.

PRIESTESSES: Immenso, immenso Fthà ... del mondo spirito animator. ...

Great, great Ptah . . . life-giving spirit of the world. ...

PRIESTS: Ah. . . .

Ah. . . .

Radames and Aida are heard against the chanting above them.

AIDA: Triste canto!

Mournful chant!

RADAMES: Il tripudio dei sacerdoti . . . .

The priests' song of jubilation. . . .

AIDA: Il nostro inno di morte. . . .

Our hymn of death. . . .

Radames tries desperately to move the stone that seals the vault.

RADAMES: Nè le mie forti braccia smuovere ti potranno, o fatal pietra!

O fatal stone, not even my strong arms can move you!

PRIESTS & PRIESTESSES: Noi t'invochiamo, t'invochiam, t'invochiam.

We invoke thee, invoke thee, invoke thee.

AIDA: Invan—tutto è finito sulla terra per noi.

In vain—on earth all is ended for us.

RADAMES: È vero! È vero!

Sadly. It is true! It is true!

AIDA: O terra addio, addio valle di pianti . . . sogno di gaudio che in dolor svanì . . . A noi si schiude, si schiude il ciel . . . si schiude il ciel e l'alme erranti volano al raggio dell'eterno dì.

Farewell, o earth, farewell vale of tears . . . dream of joy that vanished in sorrow . . . heaven is opening, is opening for us . . . heaven is opening, and our errant souls will soar to the light of eternal day.

RADAMES: O terra addio, addio valle di pianti—

Farewell, o earth, farewell vale of tears—

AIDA: O terra addio;

Farewell, o earth;

RADAMES: —sogno di gaudio che in dolor svanì—

—dream of joy that vanished in sorrow—

AIDA: —a noi si schiude—

—heaven is opening—

RADAMES: —a noi si schiude, si schiude il ciel—

—heaven is opening, is opening for us—

AIDA: —si schiude il ciel—

—is opening—

RADAMES: —si schiude il ciel e l'alme erranti—

—heaven is opening and our errant souls—

AIDA: —si schiude il ciel—

—heaven is opening—

RADAMES: —volano al raggio dell'eterno dì.

—will soar to the light of eternal day.

AIDA: —a noi si schiude il ciel.

—heaven is opening for us.

PRIESTS & PRIESTESSES: Immenso Fthà, noi t'invochiam, noi t'invochiam, t'invochiam, t'invochiam!

Great Ptah, we invoke thee, we invoke thee, invoke thee, invoke thee!

AIDA & RADAMES: Ah! . . . si schiude il ciel.

Ah! . . . heaven is opening.

Amneris, garbed in mourning robes, enters and flings herself on the stone that seals the vault.

AIDA & RADAMES: O terra addio, addio valle di pianti—

Farewell, o earth, farewell, vale of tears—

AMNERIS: Pace t'imploro—

Peace I implore of thee—

AIDA & RADAMES: —sogno di gaudio che in dolor svanì—

—dream of joy which vanished in sorrow—

AMNERIS: —salma adorata—

—adored remains—

AIDA & RADAMES: —a noi si schiude, si schiude il ciel—

—heaven is opening, is opening for us—

AMNERIS: Isi placata—

Isis appeased—

AIDA & RADAMES: —si schiude il ciel e l'alme erranti—

—heaven is opening, and our errant souls—

AMNERIS: —Isi placata ti schiuda il ciel!

May Isis appeased open heaven to you!

AIDA & RADAMES: Volano al raggio dell' eterno dì. . . .

Will soar to the light of eternal day. . . .

PRIESTS & PRIESTESSES: Noi t'invochiam, noi t'invochiam, immenso Fthà, immenso Fthà!

We invoke thee, we invoke thee, great Ptah, great Ptah!

AIDA: —il ciel—   —heaven—

RADAMES: —il ciel—   —heaven—

AIDA: —il ciel—   —heaven—

RADAMES: —il ciel—   —heaven—

AIDA & RADAMES: —si schiude   —heaven is opening . . .
il ciel . . . si schiude il ciel. heaven is opening.

Aida swoons and dies in Radames's arms.

AMNERIS: Pace t'imploro, pace   Peace I implore of thee, peace
t'imploro, pace, pace, pace.   I implore of thee, peace,
                                   peace, peace.

PRIESTS & PRIESTESSES: Im-   Great Ptah!
menso Fthà!

End of Act IV

BIBLIOGRAPHY

SOURCE OF ITALIAN LIBRETTO:
Aida by Giuseppe Verdi. Complete arrangement for voice and pianoforte by M. Saladino. London: G. Ricordi & Co., Ltd.

REFERENCE:
Biancolli, Louis. *The Opera Reader*. New York: McGraw-Hill Book Co., 1953.

Buel, James W. *The Great Operas*. London and Paris, 1899.

Filippi, Filippo. *Musica e Musicisti*. Milan, 1876. Memoirs of a leading Italian music critic who attended the 1871 Cairo première of *Aida*.

Gatti, Carlo. *Verdi, the Man and His Music*. Translated from the Italian by Elisabeth Abbott. New York: G. P. Putnam's Sons, 1955. An excellent biography stating the facts in careful chronological order.

Grout, Donald J. *A Short History of Opera*. Volume One. New York: Columbia University Press, 1947. Discussion of Verdi's music, his debt to his predecessors, and his place in operatic history.

Hurst, P. G. *The Age of Jean de Reszke*. London: Christopher Johnson, 1958.

Hussey, Dyneley. *Verdi*. "The Master Musicians" series. New York: E. P. Dutton & Co., 1940. One of the best modern Verdi biographies. Verdi's more important music is discussed in the text.

Kolodin, Irving. *The Story of the Metropolitan Opera*, 1883–1950. New York: Alfred A. Knopf, 1953.

Mapleson, James Henry. *The Mapleson Memoirs*, 1848–1888. Volume Two. Chicago, 1888.

Marek, George R. *A Front Seat at the Opera*. New York: Allen, Towne & Heath, 1948. Highly amusing, but well-authenticated, anecdotes about operas, composers and artists. The chapter on *Aida* refers to original source materials connected with the work.

Mariette, Edouard. *Mariette Pacha, Lettres et Souvenirs Personnels*. Paris, 1904.

Mariette Bey, Auguste. *The Monuments of Upper Egypt*. Translation of *Itinéraire de Haute Egypte*. London, 1877.

Monaldi, Gino. *Le Opere di Giuseppe Verdi al Teatro alla Scala* (1839–1893). Italy: G. Ricordi & Co., 1914.

Reyer, Ernest. *Notes de Musique*. Paris, 1875. Memoirs of a French composer and critic who attended the Cairo première.

Toye, Francis. *Giuseppe Verdi, His Life and Works*. New York: Alfred A. Knopf, 1946. A concise, witty, and informative biography, with a separate and comprehensive section on the operas.

Werfel, Franz and Stefan, Paul (ed.). *Verdi, the Man in His Letters*. New York: L. B. Fischer, 1942. The letters from Verdi to his librettists and the sketch of the contemporary Italian musical situation are useful.

Giuseppe Verdi, circa 1886. From the oil portrait by Boldini.

Verdi's funeral in Milan, February 27, 1901.

The Casa di Riposo for retired musicians in Milan, founded by Verdi.

CHRONOLOGICAL LIST OF VERDI'S WORKS

The following chronological list of Verdi's works is taken from *Grove's Dictionary of Music and Musicians*, Eric Blom (ed.), 5th edition, Volume VIII, pp. 745–46. The work is published by the St. Martin's Press, Inc., New York.

OPERAS: (Date and place of first performance follow opera title.)

Oberto, Conte di San Bonifacio. Nov. 17, 1839, Milan.
Un Giorno di Regno. Aug. 5, 1840, Milan.
Nabucodonosor (called *Nabucco*). Mar. 9, 1842, Milan.
I Lombardi alla prima crociata. Feb. 11, 1843, Milan.
Ernani. Mar. 9, 1844, Venice.
I due Foscari. Nov. 3, 1844, Rome.
Giovanna d'Arco. Feb. 15, 1845, Milan.
Alzira. Aug. 12, 1845, Naples.
Attila. Mar. 17, 1846, Venice.
Macbeth. Mar. 14, 1847, Florence.
I Masnadieri. July 22, 1847, London.
Jérusalem (French version of *I Lombardi*). Nov. 26, 1847, Paris.
Il Corsaro. Oct. 25, 1848, Trieste.
La Battaglia di Legnano. Jan. 27, 1849, Rome.
Luisa Miller. Dec. 8, 1849, Naples.
Stiffelio. Nov. 16, 1850, Trieste.
Rigoletto. Mar. 11, 1851, Venice.
Il Trovatore. Jan. 19, 1853, Rome.
La Traviata. Mar. 6, 1853, Venice.
Les Vêpres siciliennes. June 13, 1855, Paris.

Simon Boccanegra. Mar. 12, 1857, Venice.
Aroldo (new version of *Stiffelio*). Aug. 16, 1857, Rimini.
Un Ballo in Maschera. Feb. 17, 1859, Rome.
La Forza del Destino. Nov. 10, 1862, St. Petersburg.
Macbeth (revised). Apr. 21, 1865, Paris.
Don Carlos. Mar. 11, 1867, Paris.
Aida. Dec. 24, 1871, Cairo.
Simon Boccanegra (revised). Mar. 24, 1881, Milan.
Otello. Feb. 5, 1887, Milan.
Falstaff. Feb. 9, 1893, Milan.

SONGS:

Sei romanze (1838): "Non t'accostare all' urna." "More, Elisa, lo
    stanco poeta." "In solitaria stanza." "Nell' orror di notte
    oscura." "Perduta ho la pace." "Deh, pietosa oh addolorata."
"L'esule," a song for bass, 1839.
"La seduzione," a song for bass, 1839.
"Chi i bei dì m'adduce ancora," 1842.
Album di sei romanze, 1845: "Il tramonto." "La zingara." "Ad
    una stella." "Lo spazzocamino." "Il mistero." "Brindisi."
"Il poveretto," romanza, 1847.
"La preghiera del poeta," 1858.
"Il Brigidin," 1863.
"Stornello," 1869.
"Tu dici che non m'ami," 1869.
"Pietà, Signor," 1894.

VOCAL TRIO:

"Guarda che bianca luna," notturno a tre voci: soprano, tenor
    and bass, with flute obbligato, 1839.

CHAMBER MUSIC:

String Quartet, 1873.

SECULAR CHORAL WORKS:

"Suona la tromba," cantata, 1848.
"Inno alle nazioni," 1862. (For the London Exhibition.)

SACRED CHORAL WORKS:

Requiem for Manzoni, 1874.
Pater Noster for 5-part chorus, 1880.
Ave Maria, soprano and string acc., 1880.
Ave Maria, scala enigmatica, four parts, 1889.
Stabat Mater, chorus and orchestra. ⎱
Te Deum, double chorus and orchestra. ⎰ First performance,
Laudi alla Vergine Maria, 4-part chorus; Paris, 1898.
  on Dante's *Paradiso*.

CATALOGUE OF DOVER BOOKS

Dover Classical Records

Now available directly to the public exclusively from Dover: top-quality recordings of fine classical music for only $2 per record! Originally released by a major company (except for the previously unreleased Gimpel recording of Bach) to sell for $5 and $6, these records were issued under our imprint only after they had passed a severe critical test. We insisted upon:

First-rate music that is enjoyable, musically important and culturally significant.

First-rate performances, where the artists have carried out the composer's intentions, in which the music is alive, vigorous, played with understanding and sympathy.

First-rate sound—clear, sonorous, fully balanced, crackle-free, whir-free.

Have in your home music by major composers, performed by such gifted musicians as Elsner, Gitlis, Wührer, the Barchet Quartet, Gimpel. Enthusiastically received when first released, many of these performances are definitive. The records are not seconds or remainders, but brand new pressings made on pure vinyl from carefully chosen master tapes. "All purpose" 12" monaural 33⅓ rpm records, they play equally well on hi-fi and stereo equipment. Fine music for discriminating music lovers, superlatively played, flawlessly recorded: there is no better way to build your library of recorded classical music at remarkable savings. There are no strings; this is not a come-on, not a club, forcing you to buy records you may not want in order to get a few at a lower price. Buy whatever records you want in any quantity, and never pay more than $2 each. Your obligation ends with your first purchase. And that's when ours begins. Dover's money-back guarantee allows you to return any record for any reason, even if you don't like the music, for a full, immediate refund, no questions asked.

MOZART: STRING QUARTET IN A MAJOR (K.464); STRING QUARTET IN C MAJOR ("DISSONANT", K.465), Barchet Quartet. The final two of the famed Haydn Quartets, high-points in the history of music. The A Major was accepted with delight by Mozart's contemporaries, but the C Major, with its dissonant opening, aroused strong protest. Today, of course, the remarkable resolutions of the dissonances are recognized as major musical achievements. "Beautiful warm playing," MUSICAL AMERICA. "Two of Mozart's loveliest quartets in a distinguished performance," REV. OF RECORDED MUSIC. (Playing time 58 mins.) HCR 5200 $2.00

MOZART: QUARTETS IN G MAJOR (K.80); D MAJOR (K.155); G MAJOR (K.156); C MAJOR (K157), Barchet Quartet. The early chamber music of Mozart receives unfortunately little attention. First-rate music of the Italian school, it contains all the lightness and charm that belongs only to the youthful Mozart. This is currently the only separate source for the composer's work of this time period. "Excellent," HIGH FIDELITY. "Filled with sunshine and youthful joy; played with verve, recorded sound live and brilliant," CHRISTIAN SCI. MONITOR. (Playing time 51 mins.) HCR 5201 $2.00

MOZART: SERENADE #9 IN D MAJOR ("POSTHORN", K.320); SERENADE #6 IN D MAJOR ("SERENATA NOTTURNA", K.239), Pro Musica Orch. of Stuttgart, under Edouard van Remoortel. For Mozart, the serenade was a highly effective form, since he could bring to it the immediacy and intimacy of chamber music as well as the free fantasy of larger group music. Both these serenades are distinguished by a playful, mischievous quality, a spirit perfectly captured in this fine performance. "A triumph, polished playing from the orchestra," HI FI MUSIC AT HOME. "Sound is rich and resonant, fidelity is wonderful," REV. OF RECORDED MUSIC. (Playing time 51 mins.) HCR 5202 $2.00

MOZART: DIVERTIMENTO IN E FLAT MAJOR FOR STRING TRIO (K.563); ADAGIO AND FUGUE IN F MINOR FOR STRING TRIO (K.404a), Kehr Trio. The Divertimento is one of Mozart's most beloved pieces, called by Einstein "the finest, most perfect trio ever heard." It is difficult to imagine a music lover who will not be delighted by it. This is the only recording of the lesser known Adagio and Fugue, written in 1782 and influenced by Bach's Well-Tempered Clavichord. "Extremely beautiful recording, strongly recommended," THE OBSERVER. "Superior to rival editions," HIGH FIDELITY. (Playing time 51 mins.) HCR 5203 $2.00

SCHUMANN: KREISLERIANA (OP.16); FANTASY IN C MAJOR ("FANTASIE," OP.17), Vlado Perlemuter, Piano. The vigorous Romantic imagination and the remarkable emotional qualities of Schumann's piano music raise it to special eminence in 19th century creativity. Both these pieces are rooted to the composer's tortuous romance with his future wife, Clara, and both receive brilliant treatment at the hands of Vlado Perlemuter, Paris Conservatory, proclaimed by Alfred Cortot "not only a great virtuoso but also a great musician." "The best Kreisleriana to date," BILLBOARD. (Playing time 55 mins.) HCR 5204 $2.00

SCHUMANN: TRIO #1, D MINOR; TRIO #3, G MINOR, Trio di Bolzano. The fiery, romantic, melodic Trio #1, and the dramatic, seldom heard Trio #3 are both movingly played by a fine chamber ensemble. No one personified Romanticism to the general public of the 1840's more than did Robert Schumann, and among his most romantic works are these trios for cello, violin and piano. "Ensemble and overall interpretation leave little to be desired," HIGH FIDELITY. "An especially understanding performance," REV. OF RECORDED MUSIC. (Playing time 54 mins.) HCR 5205 $2.00

CATALOGUE OF DOVER BOOKS

SCHUMANN: TRIOS #1 IN D MINOR (OPUS 63) AND #3 IN G MINOR (OPUS 110), Trio di Bol-zano. The fiery, romantic, melodic Trio #1 and the dramatic, seldom heard Trio #3 are both movingly played by a fine chamber ensemble. No one personified Romanticism to the general public of the 1840's more than did Robert Schumann, and among his most romantic works are these trios for cello, violin and piano. "Ensemble and overall interpretation leave little to be desired," HIGH FIDELITY. "An especially understanding performance," REV. OF RE-CORDED MUSIC. (Playing time 54 mins.) HCR 5205 **$2.00**

SCHUBERT: QUINTET IN A ("TROUT") (OPUS 114), AND NOCTURNE IN E FLAT (OPUS 148), Friedrich Wührer, Piano and Barchet Quartet. If there is a single piece of chamber music that is a universal favorite, it is probably Schubert's "Trout" Quintet. Delightful melody, harmonic resources, musical exuberance are its characteristics. The Nocturne (played by Wührer, Barchet, and Reimann) is an exquisite piece with a deceptively simple theme and harmony. "The best Trout on the market—Wührer is a fine Viennese-style Schubertian, and his spirit infects the Barchets," ATLANTIC MONTHLY. "Exquisitely recorded," ETUDE. (Playing time 44 mins.) HCR 5206 **$2.00**

SCHUBERT: PIANO SONATAS IN C MINOR AND B (OPUS 147), Friedrich Wührer. Schubert's sonatas retain the structure of the classical form, but delight listeners with romantic free-dom and a special melodic richness. The C Minor, one of the Three Grand Sonatas, is a product of the composer's maturity. The B Major was not published until 15 years after his death. "Remarkable interpretation, reproduction of the first rank," DISQUES. "A superb pianist for music like this, musicianship, sweep, power, and an ability to integrate Schubert's measures such as few pianists have had since Schnabel," Harold Schonberg. (Playing time 49 mins.) HCR 5207 **$2.00**

STRAVINSKY: VIOLIN CONCERTO IN D, Ivry Gitlis, Cologne Orchestra; DUO CONCERTANTE, Ivry Gitlis, Violin, Charlotte Zelka, Piano, Cologne Orchestra; JEU DE CARTES, Bamberg Sym-phony, under Hollreiser. Igor Stravinsky is probably the most important composer of this century, and these three works are among the most significant of his neoclassical period of the 30's. The Violin Concerto is one of the few modern classics. Jeu de Cartes, a ballet score, bubbles with gaiety, color and melodiousness. "Imaginatively played and beautifully recorded," E. T. Canby, HARPERS MAGAZINE. "Gitlis is excellent, Hollreiser beautifully worked out," HIGH FIDELITY. (Playing time 55 mins.) HCR 5208 **$2.00**

GEMINIANI: SIX CONCERTI GROSSI, OPUS 3, Helma Elsner, Harpsichord, Barchet Quartet, Pro Musica Orch. of Stuttgart, under Reinhardt. Francesco Geminiani (1687-1762) has been redis-covered in the same musical exploration that revealed Scarlatti, Vivaldi, and Corelli. In form he is more sophisticated than the earlier Italians, but his music delights modern listeners with its combination of contrapuntal techniques and the full harmonies and rich melodies charcteristic of Italian music. This is the only recording of the six 1733 concerti: D Major, B Flat Minor, E Minor, G Minor, E Minor (bis), and D Minor. "I warmly recommend it, spacious, magnificent, I enjoyed every bar," C. Cudworth, RECORD NEWS. "Works of real charm, recorded with understanding and style," ETUDE. (Playing time 52 mins.) HCR 5209 **$2.00**

MODERN PIANO SONATAS: BARTOK: SONATA FOR PIANO; BLOCH: SONATA FOR PIANO (1935); PROKOFIEV, PIANO SONATA #7 IN B FLAT ("STALINGRAD"); STRAVINSKY: PIANO SONATA (1924), István Nádas, Piano. Shows some of the major forces and directions in modern piano music: Stravinsky's crisp austerity, Bartok's fusion of Hungarian folk motives; incisive di-verse rhythms, and driving power; Bloch's distinctive emotional vigor; Prokofiev's brilliance and melodic beauty couched in pre-Romantic forms. "A most interesting documentation of the contemporary piano sonata. Nadas is a very good pianist." HIGH FIDELITY. (Playing time 59 mins.) HCR 5215 **$2.00**

VIVALDI: CONCERTI FOR FLUTE, VIOLIN, BASSOON, AND HARPSICHORD: #8 IN G MINOR, #21 IN F, #27 IN D, #7 IN D; SONATA #1 IN A MINOR, Gastone Tassinari, Renato Giangrandi, Giorgio Semprini, Arlette Eggmann. More than any other Baroque composer, Vivaldi moved the concerto grosso closer to the solo concert we deem standard today. In these concerti he wrote virtuosi music for the solo instruments, allowing each to introduce new material or expand on musical ideas, creating tone colors unusual even for Vivaldi. As a result, this record displays a new area of his genius, offering some of his most brilliant music. Per-formed by a top-rank European group. (Playing time 45 mins.) HCR 5216 **$2.00**

LÜBECK: CANTATAS: HILF DEINEM VOLK; GOTT, WIE DEIN NAME, Stuttgart Choral Society, Swabian Symphony Orch.; PRELUDES AND FUGUES IN C MINOR AND IN E, Eva Hölderlin, Organ. Vincent Lübeck (1654-1740), contemporary of Bach and Buxtehude, was one of the great figures of the 18th-century North German school. These examples of Lübeck's few surviving works indicate his power and brilliance. Voice and instrument lines in the cantatas are strongly reminiscent of the organ: the preludes and fugues show the influence of Bach and Buxtehude. This is the only recording of the superb cantatas. Text and translation included. "Outstanding record," E. T. Canby, SAT. REVIEW. "Hölderlin's playing is exceptional," AM. RECORD REVIEW. "Will make [Lübeck] many new friends," Philip Miller. (Playing time 37 mins.) HCR 5217 **$2.00**

CATALOGUE OF DOVER BOOKS

DONIZETTI: BETLY (LA CAPANNA SVIZZERA), Soloists of Compagnia del Teatro dell'Opera Comica di Roma, Societa del Quartetto, Rome, Chorus and Orch. Betly, a delightful one-act opera written in 1836, is similar in style and story to one of Donizetti's better-known operas, L'Elisir. Betly is lighthearted and farcical, with bright melodies and a freshness characteristic of the best of Donizetti. Libretto (English and Italian) included. "The chief honors go to Angela Tuccari who sings the title role, and the record is worth having for her alone," M. Rayment, GRAMOPHONE REC. REVIEW. "The interpretation . . . is excellent . . . This is a charming record which we recommend to lovers of little-known works," DISQUES.
HCR 5218 **$2.00**

ROSSINI: L'OCCASIONE FA IL LADRO (IL CAMBIO DELLA VALIGIA), Soloists of Compagnia del Teatro dell'Opera Comica di Roma, Societa del Quartetto, Rome, Chorus and Orch. A charming one-act opera buffa, this is one of the first works of Rossini's maturity, and it is filled with the wit, gaiety and sparkle that make his comic operas second only to Mozart's. Like other Rossini works, L'Occasione makes use of the theme of impersonation and attendant amusing confusions. This is the only recording of this important buffa. Full libretto (English and Italian) included. "A major rebirth, a stylish performance . . . the Roman recording engineers have outdone themselves," H. Weinstock, SAT. REVIEW. (Playing time 53 mins.)
HCR 5219 **$2.00**

DOWLAND: "FIRST BOOKE OF AYRES," Pro Musica Antiqua of Brussels, Safford Cape, Director. This is the first recording to include all 22 of the songs of this great collection, written by John Dowland, one of the most important writers of songs of 16th and 17th century England. The participation of the Brussels Pro Musica under Safford Cape insures scholarly accuracy and musical artistry. "Powerfully expressive and very beautiful," B. Haggin. "The musicianly singers . . . never fall below an impressive standard," Philip Miller. Text included. (Playing time 51 mins.)
HCR 5220 **$2.00**

FRENCH CHANSONS AND DANCES OF THE 16TH CENTURY, Pro Musica Antiqua of Brussels, Safford Cape, Director. A remarkable selection of 26 three- or four-part chansons and delightful dances from the French Golden Age—by such composers as Orlando Lasso, Crecquillon, Claude Gervaise, etc. Text and translation included. "Delightful, well-varied with respect to mood and to vocal and instrumental color," HIGH FIDELITY. "Performed with . . . discrimination and musical taste, full of melodic distinction and harmonic resource," Irving Kolodin. (Playing time 39 mins.)
HCR 5221 **$2.00**

GALUPPI: CONCERTI A QUATRO: #1 IN G MINOR, #2 IN G, #3 IN D, #4 IN C MINOR, #5 IN E FLAT, AND #6 IN B FLAT, Biffoli Quartet. During Baldassare Galuppi's lifetime, his instrumental music was widely renowned, and his contemporaries Mozart and Haydn thought highly of his work. These 6 concerti reflect his great ability; and they are among the most interesting compositions of the period. They are remarkable for their unusual combinations of timbres and for emotional elements that were only then beginning to be introduced into music. Performed by the well-known Biffoli Quartet, this is the only record devoted exclusively to Galuppi. (Playing time 47 mins.)
HCR 5222 **$2.00**

HAYDN: DIVERTIMENTI FOR WIND BAND, IN C; IN F; DIVERTIMENTO A NOVE STROMENTI IN C FOR STRINGS AND WIND INSTRUMENTS, reconstructed by H. C. Robbins Landon, performed by members of Vienna State Opera Orch.; MOZART DIVERTIMENTI IN C, III (K. 187) AND IV (K. 188), Salzburg Wind Ensemble. Robbins Landon discovered Haydn manuscripts in a Benedictine monastery in Lower Austria, edited them and restored their original instrumentation The result is this magnificent record. Two little-known divertimenti by Mozart—of great charm and appeal—are also included. None of this music is available elsewhere (Playing time 58 mins.)
HCR 5223 **$2.00**

PURCELL: TRIO SONATAS FROM "SONATAS OF FOUR PARTS" (1697): #9 IN F ("GOLDEN"), #7 IN C, #1 IN B MINOR, #10 IN D, #4 IN D MINOR, #2 IN E FLAT, AND #8 IN G MINOR, Giorgio Ciompi, and Werner Torkanowsky, Violins, Geo. Koutzen, Cello, and Herman Chessid, Harpsichord. These posthumously-published sonatas show Purcell at his most advanced and mature. They are certainly among the finest musical examples of pre-modern chamber music. Those not familiar with his instrumental music are well-advised to hear these outstanding pieces. "Performance sounds excellent," Harold Schonberg. "Some of the most noble and touching music known to anyone," AMERICAN RECORD GUIDE. (Playing time 58 mins.)
HCR 5224 **$2.00**

BARTOK: VIOLIN CONCERTO; SONATA FOR UNACCOMPANIED VIOLIN, Ivry Gitlis, Pro Musica of Vienna, under Hornstein. Both these works are outstanding examples of Bartok's final period, and they show his powers at their fullest. The Violin Concerto is, in the opinion of many authorities, Bartok's finest work, and the Sonata, his last work, is "a masterpiece" (F. Sackville West). "Wonderful, finest performance of both Bartok works I have ever heard," GRAMOPHONE. "Gitlis makes such potent and musical sense out of these works that I suspect many general music lovers (not otherwise in sympathy with modern music) will discover to their amazement that they like it. Exceptionally good sound," AUDITOR. (Playing time 54 mins.)
HCR 5211 **$2.00**

J. S. BACH: PARTITAS FOR UNACCOMPANIED VIOLIN: #2 in D Minor and #3 in E, Bronislav Gimpel. Bach's works for unaccompanied violin fall within the same area that produced the Brandenburg Concerti, the Orchestral Suites, and the first part of the Well-Tempered Clavichord. The D Minor is considered one of Bach's masterpieces; the E Major is a buoyant work with exceptionally interesting bariolage effects. This is the first release of a truly memorable recording by Bronislav Gimpel, "as a violinist, the equal of the greatest" (P. Leron, in OPERA, Paris). (Playing time 53 mins.)　　　　　　HCR 5212 **$2.00**

ROSSINI: QUARTETS FOR WOODWINDS: #1 IN F, #4 IN B FLAT, #5 IN D, AND #6 IN F, N. Y. Woodwind Quartet Members: S. Baron, Flute, J. Barrows, French Horn; B. Garfield, Bassoon; D. Glazer, Clarinet. Rossini's great genius was centered in the opera, but he also wrote a small amount of first-rate non-vocal music. Among these instrumental works, first place is usually given to the very interesting quartets. Of the three different surviving arrangements, this wind group version is the original, and this is the first recording of these works. "Each member of the group displays wonderful virtuosity when the music calls for it, at other times blending sensitively into the ensemble," HIGH FIDELITY. "Sheer delight," Philip Miller. (Playing time 45 mins.)　　　　　　HCR 5214 **$2.00**

TELEMANN: THE GERMAN FANTASIAS FOR HARPSICHORD (#1-12), Helma Elsner. Until recently, Georg Philip Telemann (1681-1767) was one of the mysteriously neglected great men of music. Recently he has received the attention he deserved. He created music that delights modern listeners with its freshness and originality. These fantasias are free in form and reveal the intricacy of thorough bass music, the harmonic wealth of the "new music," and a distinctive melodic beauty. "This is another blessing of the contemporary LP output. Miss Elsner plays with considerable sensitivity and a great deal of understanding," REV. OF RECORDED MUSIC. "Fine recorded sound," Harold Schonberg. "Recommended warmly, very high quality," DISQUES. (Playing time 50 mins.)　　　　　　HCR 5210 **$2.00**

Nova Recordings

In addition to our reprints of outstanding out-of-print records and American releases of first-rate foreign recordings, we have established our own new records. In order to keep every phase of their production under our own control, we have engaged musicians of world renown to play important music (for the most part unavailable elsewhere), have made use of the finest recording studios in New York, and have produced tapes equal to anything on the market, we believe. The first of these entirely new records are now available.

RAVEL: GASPARD DE LA NUIT, LE TOMBEAU DE COUPERIN, JEUX D'EAU, Beveridge Webster, Piano. Webster studied under Ravel and played his works in European recitals, often with Ravel's personal participation in the program. This record offers examples of the three major periods of Ravel's pianistic work, and is a must for any serious collector or music lover. (Playing time about 50 minutes).　　　　　Monaural HCR 5213 **$2.00**
Stereo HCR ST 7000 **$2.00**

EIGHTEENTH CENTURY FRENCH FLUTE MUSIC, Jean-Pierre Rampal, Flute, and Robert Veyron-Lacroix, Harpsichord. Contains Concerts Royaux #7 for Flute and Harpsichord in G Minor, Francois Couperin; Sonata dite l'Inconnue in G for Flute and Harpsichord, Michel de la Barre; Sonata #6 in A Minor, Michel Blavet; and Sonata in D Minor, Anne Danican-Philidor. In the opinion of many Rampal is the world's premier flutist. (Playing time about 45 minutes)　　　　　Monaural HCR 5238 **$2.00**
Stereo HCR ST 7001 **$2.00**

SCHUMANN: NOVELLETTEN (Opus 21), Beveridge Webster, Piano. Brilliantly played in this original recording by one of America's foremost keyboard performers. Connected Romantic pieces. Long a piano favorite. (Playing time about 45 minutes)　　　　　Monaural HCR 5239 **$2.00**
Stereo HCR ST 7002 **$2.00**

Music

A GENERAL HISTORY OF MUSIC, Charles Burney. A detailed coverage of music from the Greeks up to 1789, with full information on all types of music: sacred and secular, vocal and instrumental, operatic and symphonic. Theory, notation, forms, instruments, innovators, composers, performers, typical and important works, and much more in an easy, entertaining style. Burney covered much of Europe and spoke with hundreds of authorities and composers so that this work is more than a compilation of records . . . it is a living work of careful and first-hand scholarship. Its account of thoroughbass (18th century) Italian music is probably still the best introduction on the subject. A recent NEW YORK TIMES review said, "Surprisingly few of Burney's statements have been invalidated by modern research . . . still of great value." Edited and corrected by Frank Mercer. 35 figures. Indices. 1915pp. 5⅜ x 8. 2 volumes. **T36 The Set, Clothbound $12.50**

A DICTIONARY OF HYMNOLOGY, John Julian. This exhaustive and scholarly work has become known as an invaluable source of hundreds of thousands of important and often difficult to obtain facts on the history and use of hymns in the western world. Everyone interested in hymns will be fascinated by the accounts of famous hymns and hymn writers and amazed by the amount of practical information he will find. More than 30,000 entries on individual hymns, giving authorship, date and circumstances of composition, publication, textual variations, translations, denominational and ritual usage, etc. Biographies of more than 9,000 hymn writers, and essays on important topics such as Christmas carols and children's hymns, and much other unusual and valuable information. A 200 page double-columned index of first lines — the largest in print. Total of 1786 pages in two reinforced clothbound volumes. 6¼ x 9¼. **The set, T333 Clothbound $17.50**

MUSIC IN MEDIEVAL BRITAIN, F. Ll. Harrison. The most thorough, up-to-date, and accurate treatment of the subject ever published, beautifully illustrated. Complete account of institutions and choirs; carols, masses, and motets; liturgy and plainsong; and polyphonic music from the Norman Conquest to the Reformation. Discusses the various schools of music and their reciprocal influences; the origin and development of new ritual forms; development and use of instruments; and new evidence on many problems of the period. Reproductions of scores, over 200 excerpts from medieval melodies. Rules of harmony and dissonance; influence of Continental styles; great composers (Dunstable, Cornysh, Fairfax, etc.); and much more. Register and index of more than 400 musicians. Index of titles. General Index. 225-item bibliography. 6 Appendices. xix + 491pp. 5⅝ x 8¾. **T705 Clothbound $10.00**

THE MUSIC OF SPAIN, Gilbert Chase. Only book in English to give concise, comprehensive account of Iberian music; new Chapter covers music since 1941. Victoria, Albéniz, Cabezón, Pedrell, Turina, hundreds of other composers; popular and folk music; the Gypsies; the guitar; dance, theatre, opera, with only extensive discussion in English of the Zarzuela; virtuosi such as Casals; much more. "Distinguished . . . readable," Saturday Review. 400-item bibliography. Index. 27 photos. 383pp. 5⅜ x 8. **T549 Paperbound $2.00**

ON STUDYING SINGING, Sergius Kagen. An intelligent method of voice-training, which leads you around pitfalls that waste your time, money, and effort. Exposes rigid, mechanical systems, baseless theories, deleterious exercises. "Logical, clear, convincing . . . dead right," Virgil Thomson, N.Y. Herald Tribune. "I recommend this volume highly," Maggie Teyte, Saturday Review. 119pp. 5⅜ x 8. **T622 Paperbound $1.35**

WILLIAM LAWES, M. Lefkowitz. This is the definitive work on Lawes, the versatile, prolific, and highly original "King's musician" of 17th century England. His life is reconstructed from original documents, and nearly every piece he ever wrote is examined and evaluated: his fantasias, pavans, violin "sonatas," lyra viol and bass viol suites, and music for harp and theorbo; and his songs, masques, and theater music to words by Herrick ("Gather Ye Rosebuds"), Jonson, Suckling, Shirley, and others. The author shows the innovations of dissonance, augmented triad, and other Italian influences Lawes helped introduce to England. List of Lawes' complete works and several complete scores by this major precursor of Purcell and the 18th century developments. Index. 5 Appendices. 52 musical excerpts, many never before in print. Bibliography. x + 320pp. 5⅜ x 8. **T706 Clothbound $10.00**

THE FUGUE IN BEETHOVEN'S PIANO MUSIC, J. V. Cockshoot. The first study of a neglected aspect of Beethoven's genius: his ability as a writer of fugues. Analyses of early studies and published works demonstrate his original and powerful contributions to composition. 34 works are examined, with 143 musical excerpts. For all pianists, teachers, students, and music-minded readers with a serious interest in Beethoven. Index. 93-item bibliography. Illustration of original score for "Fugue in C." xv + 212pp. 5⅝ x 8⅜. **T704 Clothbound $6.00**

CATALOGUE OF DOVER BOOKS

ROMAIN ROLLAND'S ESSAYS ON MUSIC, ed. by David Ewen. 16 best essays by great critic of our time, Nobel Laureate, discuss Mozart, Beethoven, Gluck, Handel, Berlioz, Wagner, Wolf, Saint-Saëns, Metastasio, Lully, Telemann, Grétry, "Origins of 18th Century 'Classic' Style," and musical life of 18th century Germany and Italy. "Shows the key to the high place that Rolland still holds in the world of music," Library Journal. 371pp. 5⅜ x 8.
T550 Paperbound **$1.50**

A GENERAL HISTORY OF THE SCIENCE AND PRACTICE OF MUSIC, Sir John Hawkins. Originally published in 1776, long regarded a genuine classic of musicology. Traces the origin and development of music theory, harmonic and contrapuntal processes, polyphony, musical notation, orchestration, instrumentation, etc. from earliest recorded evidence of music experiment to the author's own time, taking into account a score of musical forms—plainsong, motet, ballad, oratorio, opera, madrigal, canon, cantata, many more—and the particular contributions of various peoples. Still extremely valuable for its consideration of musical theorists and their work and detailed summaries and exact quotes from historically important works unavailable except in largest libraries. Biographical and critical information about hundreds of musicians undeservedly forgotten and now being rediscovered. A unique and significant work of music scholarship, prized by musicologists, composers, performers, historians of culture, and musical amateurs. Reproduction of 1853 edition. New introduction by Charles Cudworth, Curator, Pendlebury Library of Music, Cambridge, England. 315 illustrations; 60 full-page plates. 153 musical excerpts. 20 facsimiles of ancient manuscripts. Memoir of author. Index. Two volumes. Total of 1020pp. of text. 7⅞ x 10¾.
T1048-49 The set, Clothbound **$15.00**

THE GIFT TO BE SIMPLE, Edward Deming Andrews. Students of American history and culture, hymnologists, musicians, historians of religion, and anyone interested in reading about unusual peoples and customs will welcome this unique and authoritative account of Shaker music. Examines the origin of verses and of numerous Shaker dances; the rituals and gestures that accompanied singing; the unusual music theory developed by Shaker musicians and the melodies that were produced. Captures the spirit of an humble and devout people as expressed in many actual texts of hymns, dance songs, ritualistic songs, songs of humility, etc. Includes musical notations of about eighty melodies. A short introduction shows the development of the Shaker movement from its origins (about 1750), through the period of its greatest influence in the 1840's, to its post-Civil War decline. Index of first lines and melodies. Bibliography. 17 illustrations. ix + 170pp. 5⅜ x 8.
T22 Paperbound **$1.50**

BEETHOVEN AND HIS NINE SYMPHONIES, George Grove, editor of Grove's Dictionary of Music and Musicians. In this modern middle-level classic of musicology Grove not only analyzes all nine of Beethoven's symphonies very thoroughly in terms of their musical structure, but also discusses the circumstances under which they were written, Beethoven's stylistic development, and much other background material. This is an extremely rich book, yet very easily followed; it is highly recommended to anyone seriously interested in music. Over 250 musical passages. Index. viii + 407pp. 5⅜ x 8.
T334 Paperbound **$2.00**

AIDA BY GIUSEPPI VERDI, translated and introduced by Ellen H. Bleiler. Full handbook to the most popular opera of all; everything the operagoer (or listener) needs except the music itself. Complete Italian libretto, with all repeats, with new, modern English translation in parallel columns; biography of Verdi and librettists; background to composition of Aida; musical history; plot summary; musical excerpts; pictorial section of 76 illustrations showing Verdi, famous singers, famous performances, etc. Large clear type for easy reading. 147pp. 5⅝ x 8½.
T405 Paperbound **$1.00**

LA BOHEME BY GIACOMO PUCCINI, translated and introduced by Ellen H. Bleiler. Complete handbook for the operagoer, with everything needed for full enjoyment except the musical score itself. Complete Italian libretto, with new modern English line-by-line translation—the only libretto printing all repeats; biography of Puccini; the librettists; background to the opera, Murger's La Boheme, etc.; circumstances of composition and performances; plot summary; and pictorial section of 73 illustrations showing Puccini, famous singers and performances, etc. Large clear type for easy reading. 124pp. 5⅜ x 8½. T404 Paperbound **$1.00**

Prices subject to change without notice.

Dover publishes books on art, music, philosophy, literature, languages, history, social sciences, psychology, handcrafts, orientalia, puzzles and entertainments, chess, pets and gardens, books explaining science, intermediate and higher mathematics, mathematical physics, engineering, biological sciences, earth sciences, classics of science, etc. Write to:

Dept. catrr.
Dover Publications, Inc.
180 Varick Street, N. Y. 14, N. Y.